INSIDE LLEWY

INSIDE LLEWYN DAVIS

Ethan Coen and Joel Coen

FABER & FABER

First published in 2013
by Faber and Faber Limited
74–77 Great Russell Street
London WC1B 3DA

Published in the USA by OPUS,
a division of Subtext Inc.
44 Tower Hill Loop, Tuxedo Park
NY 10987

Typeset by Country Setting, Kingsdown, Kent CT14 8ES
Printed and bound by CPI Group (UK) Ltd, Croydon, CR0 4YY

A CIP record for this book
is available from the British Library

ISBN 978-0-571-30821-7

2 4 6 8 10 9 7 5 3 1

CONTENTS

INTRODUCTION

Elijah Wald

The Greenwich Village of Llewyn Davis is not the thriving folk scene that produced Peter, Paul and Mary and changed the world when Bob Dylan went electric. It is the folk scene in the dark ages before the hit records and big money arrived, when a small coterie of true believers traded old songs like a secret language. Most of them were kids who had grown up on the streets of New York or the prefab suburbs of Long Island and New Jersey, trying to escape the dullness and conformity of the Eisenhower 1950s. Some were college students living at home with their parents, others shared apartments in what was still the old, immigrant New York of Little Italy and the Lower East Side, where a two-person hole-in-the-wall could be had for twenty-five or thirty dollars a month.

Some details of Llewyn seem like nods to familiar figures – his Welsh name recalls Dylan, and like Phil Ochs he crashes on the couch of a singing couple named Jim and Jean. But the film catches him in the moment before Dylan and Ochs arrived in New York, when no one could have imagined the Village scene becoming the center of a folk music boom that would produce international superstars and change the course of popular music. This moment of transition – before the arrival of the 60s as we know them – was captured by one of the central figures on that scene, Dave Van Ronk, in his memoir *The Mayor of MacDougal Street*, which the Coen Brothers mined for local color and a few scenes. Llewyn is not Van Ronk, but he sings some of Van Ronk's songs and shares his background as a working-class kid who split his life between music and occasional jobs as a merchant seaman.

Llewyn also shares Van Ronk's love and respect for authentic folk music, songs and styles created by working-class people and passed on from one artist to another, polished by the ebb and flow of oral tradition. For Van Ronk's generation, that well-worn authenticity provided a profound contrast to the ephemeral confections of the pop music world, and the choice to play folk music was almost like joining a religious order – complete with a vow of poverty, since there were virtually no jobs in New York for anyone who sounded like a traditional folk artist. That would change in the early 1960s, and already there were glimmerings of the world to come – a few small clubs where people could play once in a while for tips, and little record companies that might not pay anything but at least were willing to record the real stuff. With all its difficulties, Van Ronk recalled that time with deep affection – like Llewyn he was living hand-to-mouth and sleeping on couches, but for a while he was surrounded by people for whom the music mattered more than anything else.

The Village folk scene of the late 1950s has mostly been ignored or forgotten by later fans and historians, who tend to jump from Pete Seeger and his hits with the Weavers at the beginning of the decade to Dylan's arrival in 1961. By contrast, Van Ronk recalls this as a key period in which an intimate band of young musicians shaped a new approach to folksinging, studying old records to capture the grit and rawness of Delta blues and Appalachian ballads, then finding ways to make that music express their own feelings and desires. Most of these musicians did not go on to professional careers, or even make a record. (The Kossoy Sisters were among the few to be recorded, and their 1957 album was forgotten by all but the most ardent folk fans until the Coen Brothers used its version of "I'll Fly Away" to score part of their characters' odyssey through rural Mississippi in *O Brother, Where Art Thou?*) The Village scene of the late 1950s was a world of sincere, enthusiastic amateurs, ignored by the outside world but intensely dedicated and fired by youthful optimism. Van Ronk remembered, "We had no doubt that we were the cutting edge of the folk revival – but bear in mind, we were in our late teens and early twenties, and if you do not feel you are the cutting edge at that age, there is something wrong with you. Of course we were the wave of the future – we were twenty-one!"

Looking back from the twenty-first century, it can be hard to remember how different things were in the days before the constant barrage of mass media and instant communication, and the extent to which even bright young musicians in New York City could live in their own world. The center of the Village scene in those days was not a nightclub or coffeehouse, but Washington Square Park, where singers and musicians gathered to jam on Sunday afternoons.

Van Ronk started showing up in the mid-1950s, and recalled that there would be six or seven groups playing at the same time, each with their own circle of friends and listeners. By the arch at the bottom of Fifth Avenue, a crowd of kids who had gotten into folk music at progressive summer camps and Labor Youth League get-togethers would be singing union songs they had picked up at Pete Seeger concerts or from *Sing Out!* magazine. Over by the Sullivan Street side of the square the young Zionist socialists of Hashomer Hatzair would be singing "Hava Nagila" and doing Israeli folk dances. Around the fountain, a banjo virtuoso named Roger Sprung led the first wave of urban bluegrass musicians, picking high-octane hoedowns and singing in nasal harmony.

Sprung was one of the few people on that scene who had any connection with the commercial music business: he had recorded four songs in the early 1950s with a group called the Folksay Trio, whose two other members shortly renamed themselves the Tarriers and got two top ten hits, "Cindy, Oh Cindy" and "The Banana Boat Song." A song the Tarriers recorded with Sprung, "Tom Dooley," was copied by a younger group called the Kingston Trio and topped the pop chart in 1958.

The Tarriers and Kingston Trio were part of a pop-folk trend that now tends to be remembered as hokey, lightweight silliness, and the Washington Square crowd helped shape our modern opinion. For most of the young musicians in the Village, it represented the bland conformity and commercial culture they hated and were trying to escape. As Van Ronk recalled, with typical vituperation, "We knew about the Kingston Trio and Harry Belafonte and their hordes of squeaky-clean imitators, but we felt like that was a different world that had nothing to do with us. Most of those people couldn't play worth a damn and were indifferent singers, and as far as material was concerned they were scraping the top of the barrel, singing songs that we had all learned and dropped already. It was *Sing Along with Mitch* and the *Fireside Book of Folk Songs*, performed by sophomores in paisley shirts, and it was a one hundred percent rip-off: they were ripping off the material, they were ripping off the authors, composers, collectors, and sources, and they were ripping off the public."

The pop folkies Van Ronk ridiculed might rule in suburbia and Midwestern college campuses, but they had little impact on what was heard or played in New York clubs, much less by the hardcore folkniks in Washington Square. No one on that scene remembers Roger Sprung for his near brush with the Top Forty. They remember him as an older musician who knew more than the rest of them about real Southern music, and was willing to teach anyone who cared about that style. He was in the Square every Sunday, accompanied by a fellow named Lionel Kilberg who played a home-made washtub bass, and they would have a cluster of younger players around them that over the years included pretty much all the musicians who went on to lead the urban old-time and blue-grass scenes of the 1960s. Kilberg was particularly important because he was also the person who went down to city hall each month and got the permit to play music in the Square. The permit allowed them to be there from one to five o'clock, and the permit-holder had to be physically present for the singing to be legal, so Kilberg was the one absolutely necessary participant.

Along with the folk dancers, the political singalong kids, and the bluegrassers, young soloists would sit on benches or around the fountain near the arch, playing guitars, banjos, or dulcimers and singing ballads and blues. If they were any good or had enough friends, they would be surrounded by small circles of listeners, and when someone learned a new song they would bring it down to the park and other people would pick it up. Van Ronk would normally be there singing blues, and the Kossoys, Paul Clayton, or the folk-lorist Roger Abrahams sang ballads from the British Isles or the Southern mountains. Sometimes an older, established performer like Oscar Brand or Theodore Bikel might show up, or someone might bring Woody Guthrie – he was already incapacitated by Huntington's Chorea and couldn't sing, but he would occasionally strum a few chords – or the Reverend Gary Davis, a Harlem street preacher and guitar virtuoso who was the main inspiration for a generation of young fingerpickers.

Van Ronk recalled that the ballad singers and blues people tended to hang with each other because there were not many of either, and they formed a sort of clique within the clique: "We banded to-gether for mutual support, because we didn't make as much noise as the other groups, and we hated them all – the Zionists, the summer camp kids, and the bluegrassers – every last, dead one of them. Of course, we hated a lot of people in those days."

In hindsight, those ballad and blues singers were shaping a new aesthetic that would produce people like Dylan, Ochs, Joan Baez, Joni Mitchell, and inspire the folk-rock innovations of the Lovin' Spoonful, the Byrds, the Mamas and the Papas, and Crosby, Stills, Nash, and Young. (Meanwhile a related scene was being nurtured in Britain by ballad revivalists such as Ewan MacColl – Llewyn Davis sings MacColl's "Shoals of Herring" to his aging father – and hardcore blues record collectors like the young men who became the Rolling Stones.) But in the late 1950s they did not know they were on the cusp of a new era, and if anyone had told them they were sowing the seeds of a future pop or rock trend most of them would have been horrified. As Alan Lomax said, welcoming viewers to a filmed jam session in his fifth-floor walk-up apartment, "You're in Greenwich Village now, where people come to get away from America." They were a small band of true believers, outside the mainstream not only of American commercial culture, but of any mainstream, and they were proud of their independence and their secret knowledge.

Van Ronk wryly dubbed his crowd the "neo-ethnics," and to some extent they were a folk equivalent of the "early music" movement happening at the same time in the classical world – it makes perfect sense that when Llewyn Davis visits an older academic couple, the other guests include a man who plays harpsichord in a group called Musica Anticha. As in the classical world, there were famous concert artists who played in places like Carnegie and Town Hall, and then there were the young, fervent disciples searching out rare, old material and trying to play it "authentically," the way it would have sounded in its original time and place. Several of the Washington Square regulars were pursuing degrees in folklore and some made trips down South in search of old musicians and scratchy 78s. For those who remained in New York, the bible was a set of six LPs that had been assembled by a beatnik eccentric named Harry Smith and issued on the Folkways label in 1952 as *The Anthology of American Folk Music*. Compiled from recordings made for the "Race" and hillbilly markets in the 1920s, the *Anthology* introduced them to artists like Mississippi John Hurt and the banjo player Dock Boggs, and the neo-ethnics assiduously imitated every quirk and nuance of what they regarded as the real, raw antithesis of the pap purveyed by the pop folkies.

Van Ronk recalled that a lot of people listened to that set so many times that they knew every song on all six albums: "We did not like everything on those records, but it was all important to us because it showed us what was out there and how it really sounded, from the sources rather than from second- and third-hand interpreters. It changed everything, because the previous generation had liked folk songs, but sang them like trained concert singers. For us, what mattered was authenticity, reproducing the traditional ethnic styles all the way down to getting the accents right. It did not matter whether you were ethnic à la Furry Lewis, or à la Jimmie Rodgers, or a la Earl Scruggs; that was a matter of personal taste. But that it should all be authentically ethnic was a matter of principle."

As in any sect, some people were more orthodox than others. Van Ronk, like Ramblin' Jack Elliott before him and Bob Dylan a couple of years later, worked hard to get the rough, raspy vocal styles of the mountains and prairies, but other singers were willing to compromise at least a little with modern, urban tastes. Most of the women on the scene sang in lovely, clear sopranos, sometimes adopting a Southern accent but rarely striving to sound like aged farmwives. But they still studied old records and collections of ancient ballads published by academic archivists, and mastered archaic instruments like the Appalachian dulcimer.

Of all the early neo-ethnics, Paul Clayton was the most successful at combining scholarship and performance. (A handsome, bearded man, he also looked a bit like Justin Timberlake's Jim Berkey.) Clayton had a degree in folklore and had traveled around the South interviewing and recording older musicians, discovering artists like the black fingerpicker Etta Baker and the medicine show bluesman Pink Anderson. He was also the most successful performer in the clique of true believers: while the others were lucky to record a song or two on various folk compilations, he made fifteen solo LPs in the six years from 1954 to 1959. But he was not part of the pop-folk world, people like the Weavers, the Tarriers, and Harry Belafonte who were adapting traditional songs into pseudo-folk hits like "Goodnight, Irene" and "The Banana Boat Song." His albums were mostly on Folkways Records, a small, independent label that made the bulk of its profits by selling to libraries and universities. As Van Ronk recalled, "Every time Paul needed a few bucks he would hunt up some obscure folklore collection, then go see Moe Asch at Folkways and say, 'You know, Moe, I was just looking through your catalog, and I noticed that you don't have a single album of Maine lumberjack ballads . . .'

"Moe would say, 'Well, I guess that's a pretty serious omission. Do you know anyone who can sing enough of those to make a record?'

"And Paul would say, 'Well, as it happens . . .'"

Clayton's album titles give an idea of the result: along with *Timber-r-r! Lumberjack Folk Songs and Ballads*, they include *Wanted for Murder: Songs of Outlaws and Desperados*, *Bay State Ballads*, *Cumberland Mountain Folksongs*, and *Whaling and Sailing Songs from the Days of Moby Dick*. But along with the serious folklore, he also reshaped some old songs for his concert performances, writing new verses and reworking melodies, and even recorded a couple of these creations with semi-pop arrangements. None of them attracted much attention beyond the local folk scene, but his influence went a long way: a song he recorded in 1959 called "Who's Gonna Buy You Ribbons" was the inspiration for Bob Dylan's "Don't Think Twice, It's All Right."

> I'm walking down that long, lonesome road,
> You're the one that made me travel on . . .
> So it ain't no use to sit and sigh now, darlin',
> And it ain't no use to sit and cry now.
> It ain't no use to sit and wonder why, darlin',
> Just wonder who's gonna buy you ribbons when I'm gone.

If few people remember Clayton today, that is a reminder of how completely the scene changed in the few years between the late 1950s and the early 1960s. The neo-ethnics never expected to become stars – if they had nurtured any dreams of commercial success they would not have devoted themselves to folk music. In retrospect it is easy to see the Village scene of the late 1950s as a training ground for the big time, and it certainly was a hotbed of youthful enthusiasm and musical dedication, remembered by many of its denizens as their equivalent of Paris in the 1920s. But a look at the *Village Voice*'s club and coffeehouse listings puts those memories in perspective. There were some folksingers there, but they are rarely the top-billed names, and they were competing with a lot of other music. In October of 1961, when Dylan got his big break at Folk City – the only New York folk club of that period that had a liquor license, and the model for the bar in *Llewyn Davis* – it was as opening act for a local bluegrass band, the Greenbriar Boys. There were only two other clubs in town advertising any folk-singers by name, and both featured older cabaret-style performers rather than members of the young Village crowd. Meanwhile, the main rooms were sticking to jazz: Thelonious Monk, Ornette Coleman, Zoot Sims, Horace Silver, Herbie Mann – and as a reminder of how fast the times would soon be changing, Silver and Mann were on a double bill with Aretha Franklin as the opening act. (That was not particularly unusual: two months earlier, Aretha was in the same club opening for the John Coltrane Quintet.)

As for the coffeehouse where Dylan made his New York debut, the Cafe Wha?, its advertisement named no individual performers, but just showed a picture of a beatnik in beret, beard, and sunglasses and listed the entertainment as "folk singing, comedy, calypso, poetry, and congas" in "Greenwich Village's Swingingest Coffee House." The Wha? was an out-and-out tourist trap, run by a smart hustler named Manny Roth whose showbiz savvy would be passed on to his nephew David Lee Roth of Van Halen. Its regular performers included Richie Havens, Fred Neil and Karen Dalton, now recalled as folk legends, but it made the overhead by pulling in audiences of out-of-town tourists who had come to gawk at the beatniks and weirdos.

The Village's first full-time folk club, the Cafe Bizarre, had set the pattern back in 1957. Van Ronk played there on opening night and remembered, "it was selling the squares a Greenwich Village that had never existed. The ambience was cut-rate Charles Addams haunted house: dark and candlelit, with fake cobwebs hanging all over everything. The waitresses were got up to look like Morticia, with fishnet stockings, long straight hair, and so much mascara that they looked like raccoons." It was a Hollywood notion of beatnik life, as shown in movies like *Bell, Book, and Candle* where witches and warlocks mixed with beat poets and no one could tell the differ-ence, or in TV shows like *Dobie Gillis* and *Peter Gunn*. For a while the *Voice* even ran a weekly ad for a "Rent-a-Beatnik" service that would send a bearded, bereted hipster to liven up the dullest party.

In the context of the 1950s it did not take much to be typed as a beatnik weirdo. Llewyn Davis's beard would have been enough to make most right-thinking Americans giggle and point at him – compared to the crew cuts and button-down shirts of normal young people, it was the temporal equivalent of facial tattoos and multiple piercings. For an older generation that had lived through the Depression and two world wars and now was relaxing in the safety of the steadiest economic boom the American middle class has ever known, the only explanations for choosing a life of sleeping on floors and devoting one's days to obscure poetry and archaic music were insanity or perversion. Meanwhile, to the young Villagers, the older tourists represented the conformist mindlessness that had produced the McCarthy witch-hunts and the Cold War and was threatening the world with atomic Armageddon. The two groups were divided by a wall of mutual fear and mistrust, and to add insult to injury when the conventional older Americans showed up in the Village they acted like the whole place was a kind of absurd amusement park, and treated anyone who was trying to be a serious artist as part of the crazy show.

The Bizarre and the Wha? were particularly obvious about catering to the tourist trend, but even the less gaudy clubs were tough rooms to work. While the bars had to close at one a.m., the coffeehouses stayed open as long as they had customers, so performers often played five or six sets a night, seven nights a week. The crowds were rowdy, the money often just came from a tip basket, and the pace was grueling, but as a result the Village was a unique training ground. Van Ronk grumbled about the audiences and the exploitation, but also argued that those clubs taught his generation lessons they could not have learned anywhere else, balancing their devotion to unpopular ethnic styles and explaining how people like Dylan and Ochs became the best singer-songwriters in the country within a year or two of arriving. "We had so much opportunity to try out our stuff in public, get clobbered, figure out what was wrong, and go back and try it again. It was brutally hard work, because these crowds of tourists usually started out at the bars and by the time they got around to us they were completely loaded. So we would be playing for audiences of fifty or a hundred drunken suburbanites who really could not have cared less about the music – they were there to see the freaks and raise some hell. In that kind of situation, you either learn how to handle yourself onstage or you go into some other line of work, and the people who stuck it out became thoroughly seasoned pros."

The musicians who gathered in Washington Square were inspired by a shared devotion to authentic, honest music with deep history in a mythic rural America, but the club scene was driven by harsh economic realities. The New York cabaret laws were among the strictest in the country, and the only reason a lot of clubs booked folksingers was that it was a way around the regulations: an "incidental music" clause designed for restaurant background music made an exception for groups that had less than four people and did not include wind, brass or percussion instruments. That meant a club could feature poets or folksingers without meeting the arcane licensing strictures and high fees required for jazz groups, and that was particularly attractive when they began serving an audience of tourists who didn't care about the music anyway.

In some ways this situation worked to the folksingers' benefit, but along with making the clubs less than perfect concert rooms it also provided fuel for old prejudices. The tourists tended to lump folksingers and beatniks together, but when Van Ronk talked about the people his crowd hated, the beatniks were only a few steps behind the suburban squares and once again the dislike was mutual: "The beats liked cool jazz, bebop, and hard drugs, and hated folk music, which to them was all these fresh-faced kids sitting around on the floor and singing songs of the oppressed masses. When a folksinger would take the stage between two beat poets, all the finger-poppin' mamas and daddies would do everything but hold their noses. Then, when the beat poets would get up and begin to rant, all the folk fans would do likewise."

Van Ronk was not talking about the older beats – to someone who dreamed of being a rambling hobo with a guitar slung over his shoulder, Jack Kerouac's *On the Road* went right along with Woody Guthrie's songs – but by 1960 that generation was no longer reciting in the coffeehouses and the young beatniks tended to be local, middle-class kids like the folkies, who dressed like parodies of urban Bohemians and listened to ridiculous poems. As for the beats' opinion of the folk crowd, it was a mix of the contempt avant-garde outsiders have for fresh-faced do-gooders and the contempt jazz aficionados had for those who sang droning ballads and only knew three chords. The character played by John Goodman in *Llewyn Davis* is loosely inspired by the songwriter Doc Pomus, a Jewish New Yorker who earned his stripes in the 1940s singing blues in black nightclubs, and his reaction to Llewyn is typical of most jazz fans and serious hipsters on that scene: "What'd you say you play? *Folk* songs? I thought you said you were a musician."

The famous slogan of the 1960s, "Don't trust anybody over thirty," reflected a generational split that in some ways was even more important than the musical divides. For Van Ronk or Llewyn Davis, people like Pomus and Thelonious Monk might be respected as artists and Bohemian predecessors but nonetheless were part of a different world – even though that world was barely a block away. To complicate matters, that older world included most of the people who might record or hire them. Moe Asch of Folkways Records, the model for the movie's Mel, was fifty-five years old in 1960 and had recorded Woody Guthrie, Pete Seeger, and Lead Belly, as well as jazz artists like Sidney Bechet and Art Tatum. He genuinely loved traditional folk music and was a political comrade of the "old left" and an early supporter of the new protest song movement, but he was also a hard-nosed, old-fashioned businessman. His records formed the foundation of the neo-ethnic aesthetic, but most of them only reached a small base of cognoscenti, and he subsidized his less profitable projects by being famously stingy with the artists who sold better – as well as being painfully honest with borderline cases like the fictional Llewyn who didn't sell as well as they hoped.

Albert Grossman, model for the movie's Bud Grossman, was only thirty-four in 1960, but likewise was regarded by Van Ronk's generation as a member of the old guard. He had opened Chicago's Gate of Horn in 1956 as a kind of folk nightclub – it had a liquor license and hired artists the neo-ethnics regarded as "cabaret folksingers," people like Josh White, Bob Gibson, Odetta, and the Clancy Brothers, who sang folk material but presented themselves as experienced entertainers. In the 1960s Grossman would move to New York and become an icon of big-money folk promotion, first creating Peter, Paul and Mary, then managing Dylan's transformation from a waifish, guitar-strumming poet into a rock star. But even in the late 1950s, when he was just a nightclub owner,

Van Ronk's crowd tended to dismiss the cabaret style he promoted as slick and fake. The young neo-ethnics tried not to do anything that seemed like professional entertainment. They sang in rough, countrified accents, went onstage in street clothes, and presented their songs with stolid seriousness: In Van Ronk's words, "If you weren't staring into the sound-hole of your instrument, we thought you should at least have the decency and self-respect to stare at your shoes." There was a dedicated virtue and honor in this approach – it was similar to what Miles Davis was doing at the same time in jazz, turning his back to the audience so that his listeners were forced to concentrate on the music rather than the visuals – but it made no sense to club owners like Grossman, who balanced their affection for the music with a keen sense of the bottom line. As a result, Grossman never hired the young New Yorkers at the Gate – and Llewyn suffers a variation of Van Ronk's humiliating audition there.

In 1960 nobody who knew the music business and wanted to make a living had any interest in people who sounded like Van Ronk or Dylan. The top folk stars were people with nice voices who dressed like successful pop or classical musicians: Belafonte and Josh White in tailored silk shirts; the Kingston Trio in matching collegiate casual wear; and older artists like the Weavers, the Rooftop Singers, and the Limelighters, in suits and ties or evening gowns. Dylan described the dominant attitude in one of his first songs, "Talking New York," quoting a club owner telling him, "You sound like a hillbilly. We want folksingers here."

Folk City's owner, Mike Porco, the real-life counterpart of the movie's charmingly cynical Pappi Corsicato, was an exception, but that was because he knew nothing about the music business. He was just a local Italian guy who ran a bar called Gerde's on a block of factory loft buildings. His main customers were people working in the area, so he did not have a lot of nighttime business and was interested when Izzy Young, who ran a little book and record store called the Folklore Center on MacDougal Street, proposed hosting concerts there. Young was a hardcore traditionalist who had gotten into the scene by doing folk dancing and boasted that his store had the most complete selection of obscure books on world folklore in the United States. The Folklore Center was also a kind of clubhouse for the neo-ethnic crowd – Dylan wrote in

Chronicles that he wandered in on his first visit to the Village and met Van Ronk there – and when Young started his evening club in Porco's bar, he meant it to be a showcase for older, "authentic" performers like Reverend Gary Davis and young locals like Van Ronk and Clayton.

That was in January of 1960, and Young ran the club as a non-profit for five months before Porco realized that it was attracting a regular crowd and could be turned into a business. He took over the booking, renamed the place Gerde's Folk City, and for a while it was the one bar that regularly featured folksingers. That made it a step up financially from the coffeehouses, many of which just paid performers a portion of what people put in the tip basket. But like the bar in *Llewyn Davis*, it was not necessarily a quiet, serious music club. Van Ronk recalled many cheerfully raucous evenings hanging out with Porco and his friends, talking over the poor guys and gals who were trying to sing onstage: "As in most music bars, the people seated in front knew that they were watching a show but the people at the bar would act like they were in another room. When that place was crowded, it was one of the toughest rooms I have ever seen."

If one wanted to date *Inside Llewyn Davis* precisely, the obvious bookends are the opening of Folk City in January 1960, and Dylan's arrival in New York almost exactly a year later. That was a kind of in-between moment, when the scene was obviously changing but no one had any clear idea where it was headed. By the time Folk City was solidly established, the Cafe Bizarre had been open for three years and had been joined by the Cafe Wha?, the Commons, and the Gaslight Cafe, all within a block of each other on or near MacDougal Street and featuring folk music alongside a declining wave of beat poets. More clubs would open over the next few years, till at one point there were almost three dozen within a few blocks, but even in 1960 there was enough work that young musicians were drifting in from all over the country. By the time Dylan arrived from Minnesota, the core of local folk disciples had already been augmented by Carolyn Hester from Texas, Len Chandler from Ohio, and Tom Paxton, model for the movie's Troy Nelson, from Oklahoma. Like the Coens' character, Paxton started playing in the Village on weekends while doing his military service at Fort Dix, and he was a new kind of folksinger. His interest was less in learning old songs than in carrying on the tradition by writing new ones – in the movie, Nelson sings Paxton's "The Last Thing on My Mind" – and he was a key figure in the evolution from neo-ethnics to singer-songwriters.

That evolution has gotten most of the historical attention, thanks to Dylan, Paul Simon, Joni Mitchell, Leonard Cohen, and the other poetic wordsmiths who gravitated to the Village in the next few years, mixing the musical aesthetic of the folk crowd with the literary aesthetic of the beats. It was not an instant shift: when Izzy Young sponsored Dylan's first concert at Carnegie Recital Hall in November, 1961, Dylan had gotten a rave review in the *New York Times* and a contract with Columbia Records, but still attracted barely fifty listeners. His nasal voice and whining harmonica were too raw and abrasive for mainstream music fans, and even after Peter, Paul and Mary made "Blowin in the Wind" a national hit two years later, nobody could imagine him becoming a pop star in his own right. When his own performing career finally took off, he sounded as baffled as a lot of his old friends on MacDougal Street: "I once thought the biggest I could ever hope to get was like Van Ronk, but it's bigger than that now, ain't it. Yeah man, it's bigger than that. Scary as all shit."

A lot of viewers will probably think of *Inside Llewyn Davis* as an early glimpse of Dylan's kingdom. But it is more accurate to recognize it as a portrait of a smaller and quite different world that was already ending by the time Dylan showed up. Most of the singers and players who were on the Village scene in 1959 or 1960 did not evolve into the folk stars of the next decade. With the exception of Van Ronk and the New Lost City Ramblers, they were swept away by the wave of out-of-town talent or lost interest when the scene shifted from a righteous cult of folk devotees to a commercial circus. The feeling of camaraderie, of being a small band of true believers sleeping on each other's couches and swapping songs till dawn, was replaced by dreams of stardom. A lot of terrific music was made in the Village after 1960 – arguably much better music than had been made before – but it was now the center of a national and international trend. Within a few years the intimate Greenwich Village where all the singers knew each other, sang and played with each other, sometimes slept with each other and broke each other's hearts, already felt in some ways as ancient and far away as the sharecroppers' shacks of the Mississippi Delta and the hamlets of Appalachia had seemed to Van Ronk and his young peers in Washington Square.

Elijah Wald is a musician and writer who spent much of his teens sleeping on Dave Van Ronk's couch near the corner of Fourth Street and Seventh Avenue, and co-authored The Mayor of MacDougal Street.

Inside Llewyn Davis

SONGS

Hang Me, Oh Hang Me
(traditional; arr. Oscar Isaac and T Bone Burnett)
Oscar Isaac

Fare Thee Well (Dink's Song)
(traditional; arr. Marcus Mumford, Oscar Isaac and T Bone Burnett)
Oscar Isaac and Marcus Mumford
Chris Eldridge: acoustic guitar; Marcus Mumford: acoustic guitar;
Chris Thile: mandolin; Gabe Witcher: fiddle

The Last Thing on my Mind
(Tom Paxton)
Stark Sands, with Punch Brothers
Chris Eldridge: guitar; Paul Kowert: bass; Noam Pikelny: banjo;
Chris Thile: mandolin; Gabe Witcher: fiddle
T Bone Burnett: guitar; Colin Linden: guitar

Five Hundred Miles
(Hedy West)
Justin Timberlake, Carey Mulligan and Stark Sands
T Bone Burnett: guitar; David Mansfield: guitar and fiddle;
Marcus Mumford: guitar

Please, Mr. Kennedy
(Ed Rush, George Cromarty, T Bone Burnett, Justin Timberlake,
Joel Coen and Ethan Coen)
Justin Timberlake, Carey Mulligan and Stark Sands
T Bone Burnett: guitar; David Mansfield: guitar and fiddle;
Marcus Mumford: guitar

Green, Green Rocky Road
(Len Chandler and Robert Kaufman)
Oscar Isaac

The Death of Queen Jane
(music by Dáithí Sproule; lyrics traditional)
Oscar Isaac

The Shoals of Herring
(Ewan MacColl)
Oscar Isaac, with Punch Brothers
Chris Eldridge: guitar; Paul Kowert: bass; Noam Pikelny: banjo;
Chris Thile: mandolin; Gabe Witcher: fiddle

The Auld Triangle
(Brendan Behan)
Chris Thile, Chris Eldridge, Marcus Mumford,
Justin Timberlake and Gabe Witcher

Hang Me, Oh Hang Me
(traditional; arr. Oscar Isaac and T Bone Burnett)

CAST AND CREW

Inside Llewyn Davis was first shown
at the Cannes Film Festival on May 19, 2013

A Studiocanal Presentation in Association
with Anton Capital Entertainment

PRINCIPAL CAST

LLEWYN DAVIS	Oscar Isaac
JEAN	Carey Mulligan
ROLAND TURNER	John Goodman
JOHNNY FIVE	Garrett Hedlund
BUD GROSSMAN	F. Murray Abrham
JIM	Justin Timberlake
TROY NELSON	Stark Sands
AL CODY	Adam Driver
JOY	Jeanine Serralles
PAPPI CORSICATO	Max Casella
MITCH GORFEIN	Ethan Phillips
LILLIAN GORFEIN	Robin Bartlett

PRINCIPAL CREW

Written and Directed by	Joel Coen and Ethan Coen
Produced by	Scott Rudin
	Ethan Coen
	Joel Coen
Executive Producers	Robert Graf
	Olivier Courson
	Ron Halpern
Associate Producers	Catherine Farrell
	Eli Bush
Director of Photography	Bruno Delbonnel
Edited by	Roderick Jaynes
Production Designer	Jess Gonchor
Costumes Designed by	Mary Zophres
Executive Music Producer	T Bone Burnett
Supervising Sound Editor	Skip Lievsay
Casting Director	Ellen Chenoweth

FADE IN TITLE CARD

New York City 1961

Fade out.

Black.

Hard cut to a singer accompanying himself on guitar, performing "I've Been All Around This World." He is Llewyn Davis. He is spotlit, seated on the small stage of a New York club, maybe the Gaslight.

HANG ME, OH HANG ME

Hang me, oh hang me, I'll be dead and gone
Hang me, oh hang me, I'll be dead and gone
I wouldn't mind the hanging, it's just the laying in the
    grave so long
Poor boy, I've been all around this world

I've been all around Cape Jerdo and parts of Arkansas
All around Cape Jerdo and parts of Arkansas
I got so goddamn hungry I could hide behind a straw
Poor boy, I've been all around this world

I went up on a mountain, there I made my stand
I went up on a mountain, there I made my stand
Rifle on my shoulder and the dagger in my hand
Poor boy, I've been all around this world

So put the rope around my neck, hang me up so high
Put the rope around my neck, they hanged me up so high
The last words I heard them say, it won't be long now
    before you die
Poor boy, I've been all around this world

He finishes the song to applause.

LLEWYN

You've probably heard that one before, but what the hell. If it was never new, and it never gets old, then it's a folk song.

9

AT THE BAR

Pappi Corsicatto, the Greenwich Village-Italian owner of the club, nods Llewyn over. He is broadly smiling.

> PAPPI
> Boy, you were some mess last night.

> LLEWYN
> Yeah, sorry, Pappi. I'm an asshole.

> PAPPI
> Oh I don't give a shit. It's just music. Your friend is out back.

> LLEWYN
> My friend?

> PAPPI
> Guy in a suit?

A clatter offscreen attracts Llewyn's attention.

Backlit in the smoky spotlight someone with a battered guitar is just sitting down onstage.

BACK ALLEY

The steel door of the club swings open and Llewyn emerges. A thin, angular Man, older than Llewyn, in a suit a size too big, is leaning against the far wall of the alley smoking a cigarette. He studies Llewyn for a beat, then, in a Kentucky accent:

> MAN
> You a funny boy, huh?

> LLEWYN
> What?

The Man tosses the cigarette away and pushes himself off the wall.

> MAN
> Had to open ya big mouth, funny boy?

> LLEWYN
> Had to – what? It's what I do. For a living. Who're –

MAN

What ya do? Make fun a folks up there? Folks up there sangin?

LLEWYN

I'm sorry, *what*? I'm – oof!

The man has just socked him in the mouth.

MAN

You sit there in the audience last night yellin yer crap?

Llewyn is holding his mouth.

LLEWYN

Oh for Christ's sake. You yell stuff, it's a show.

MAN

Wasn't your show!

He hits him again and Llewyn goes down in the slush of the alleyway.

LLEWYN

It's not the opera, jackass!

The man kicks. Llewyn curls into a defensive ball and bellows from behind protective forearms:

It's a fucking baskethouse!

The man kicks again.

                    MAN
We leavin this fuckin cesspool. You kin have it, smartass.

GORFEINS' HALLWAY — DAY

Tracking.

We are pushing forward at floor level along a hallway, dimly daylit from the room in the background that it opens into.

Music enters at the cut, an Italian tenor, singing opera. The music has some perspective: a record playing in another apartment, perhaps, down an airshaft.

A cat's feet enter frame and it leads the continuing push-in.

The cat enters the background room, camera keeping pace. The cat veers to one side bringing into frame the bottom of a sofa. The arm of someone above frame asleep on the couch lolls down onto the floor. We can hear the sleeper's heavy breathing.

The cat leaps up, leaving frame.

Close on the sleeper: Llewyn Davis, lying on his back. At the sound of a soft impact he lets out a startled grunt and his eyes open. He blinks.

He looks down the length of his body, chin digging into chest.

His point of view: the cat stands on his chest staring back, purring with a loud rhythmic rumble.

Llewyn raises a hand to swipe the cat away.

As we hear the cat padding around the room we cut wider on Llewyn. He stirs and rises, swinging his feet out. He is in his undies.

The walls in this den are decorated with masks and totems and other naive early-civilization art.

Llewyn sits gazing stupidly about for a beat.

He reaches for pants, plops them into his lap.

He looks down at the end table just off the sofa arm. On it, some change and three subway tokens, which he swipes into an open hand and dumps into one pants pocket. Also on the table, a wallet. He thumbs open the bill compartment. It contains three dollars.

Close on him as he looks, then flips the wallet shut and shoves it into another pocket.

DOWN A HALL

We are looking down the length of a darkish hallway giving onto the brighter den.

Llewyn's head appears at the far end as he cranes to peer down the hall. He stares out for a still beat.

LLEWYN

. . . Hello?

No answer.

Llewyn relaxes, enters the hall, walks toward us in his underwear. The cat crosses the room behind him.

LIVING ROOM

Llewyn enters and bends with an oomph to pull his guitar out of a case.

He sits on a sofa, experimenting idly with chords till he finds his way into the continuing opera. He accompanies it through a couple of chord changes, humming. He loudly clears phlegm.

KITCHEN

Eggs are cracked into a bowl.

Wider: Llewyn, still undied, whisks the eggs.

After a long beat of vigorous whisking he looks about, pulls open a drawer, doesn't see what he is after. He looks around, lost, at all the cabinetry.

HALLWAY

Llewyn walks down the hall forking scrambled egg from a plate to his mouth, idly looking at the pictures on the walls.

LIVING ROOM AGAIN

Llewyn stands, mouth agape, before a shelf of records, running a finger along the frayed cardboard spines of the record jackets. The plate of eggs, empty now, sits abandoned on the hi-fi cabinet next to him.

He lands on a record, pulls it out. He looks at the sleeve with a half-smile, slips out the LP, puts it on the hi-fi spindle.

FOYER — MINUTES LATER

"Dink's Song" issues from the hi-fi, sung by a harmonizing male duo.

Dressed now, wearing a corduroy sport coat, Llewyn is hunched at a sideboard, scribbling something onto scratch paper:

> Thanks for the couch. I was a sorry mess last night.

He signs: "Ll."

COMMON HALLWAY

"Dink's Song" continues to play, now as score.

FARE THEE WELL (DINK'S SONG)

If I had wings like Nora's dove
I'd fly the river to the one I love
Fare thee well, my honey
Fare thee well

I had a man who was long and tall
Moved his body like a cannonball
Fare thee well, my honey
Fare thee well

I remember one evening in the pouring rain
And in my heart was an aching pain
Fare thee well, my honey
Fare thee well

Muddy river is muddy and wild
Can't give a bloody for my unborn child
Fare thee well, my honey
Fare thee well

Sure as a bird flying high above
Life ain't worth living without the one you love
Fare thee well, my honey
Fare thee well

Llewyn is just exiting the apartment, guitar case in hand. The hallway is a small space with only one other apartment door giving onto it; there is also an elevator.

As Llewyn leaves, the cat tries to accompany him.

A grunt from Llewyn. He tries awkwardly to hook the cat with a foot as it goes by; he fails. The purring cat runs to the far end of the hallway.

Llewyn hops after it, setting down his guitar case. One step into pursuit he hears the apartment door close – solidly – behind him.

LLEWYN

Shit.

He turns back to the door, tries the knob which he knows will not turn. And it does not: locked.

. . . Goddamnit.

The cat is winding around the legs of a small table in the hallway. Llewyn reaches for it; it eludes him; he hems it in with one waving hand and corrals it with the other.

He straightens with the cat, looks around the small space.

He goes to the neighbors' apartment door and knocks.

A beat.

. . . Hello?

Another knock; more silence.

He pushes the elevator call button.

15

While waiting, he pointlessly tries the first apartment door again.

We hear the elevator arriving, a cage door being slid. The outer door is opened by the attendant.

Llewyn grabs his guitar and steps in.

Hi . . . Could you, could I leave this cat with you?

INSIDE THE ELEVATOR

The attendant closes the doors and sets the car in motion.

ATTENDANT
With me?

LLEWYN
Yeah, I, it's the Gorfeins' cat. Just till one of them gets back.

ATTENDANT
With *me*?

LLEWYN
It just slipped out, I don't have the key. If you could just keep it till they get back?

ATTENDANT
I have to run the elevator.

LLEWYN
That's not a problem, is it? It's the Gorfeins'.

ATTENDANT
I have to run the elevator.

ADDRESS BOOK

It is being held open: a well-worn address book with sloppy entries faded to different degrees, some made in pencil, some in ink.

We hear ringing filtered through a phone line.

Wider shows Llewyn standing in a phone booth with the handset wedged between shoulder and ear, one hand holding the address book and the other hugging the cat to his chest.

City traffic rumbles by in the background, and people walk by in winter wear all heavier than Llewyn's corduroy coat.

The ringing is cut off by a female voice:

> VOICE

Sociology.

> LLEWYN

Professor Gorfein, please.

> VOICE

He's in a lecture, could I take a message?

> LLEWYN

Yeah, could you tell him, don't worry, Llewyn has the cat.

> VOICE

Llewyn is . . . the cat.

> LLEWYN

Llewyn *has* the cat. I'm Llewyn. I have his cat.

SUBWAY ENTRANCE

"Dink's Song," dipped for the preceding dialog, comes back full for this credit sequence.

An Upper West Side sidewalk subway entrance. Llewyn descends, guitar case in one hand, cat hugged to his chest.

SUBWAY STATION

Turnstile.

Guitar hoisted over it.

SUBWAY CAR

Llewyn in the middling crowded train, seated, body jiggling with the motion of the car. He looks:

A strap-hanging businessman in overcoat and narrow-brimmed fedora holds a folded-back newspaper, not reading it. He is staring at lightly dressed, cat-hugging Llewyn.

Back to Llewyn. An eye shift.

Two black kids, probably on their way to school, also staring at him.

Back to Llewyn. The cat jumps free.

Llewyn leaps up and crouch-hustles after it. People make way for cat and pursuing man, giving looks.

WEST 4TH STREET EXIT

Another sidewalk subway access. Llewyn emerges, the recovered cat once again held to his chest.

VILLAGE STREETS

Llewyn walks, guitar in hand, cat to chest.

EXT. BERKEY'S APARTMENT BUILDING

As the credits end Llewyn turns into a tenement building halfway up the street.

TENEMENT BUILDING / FOYER

Llewyn scans the tenant list and presses the buzzer for BERKEY 6C. No answer. He presses the button for SUPER 1C.

INSIDE

Llewyn is buzzed in. An older Italian man in a wifebeater and blue work pants cinched high on his midriff cracks open a door at the end of the hall.

LLEWYN

Hey, Nunzio.

NUNZIO
Yeah, they ain't home though.

LLEWYN
It's okay, I know. Can I use the fire escape?

BERKEY APARTMENT

As Llewyn tops the fire-escape stairs on the sixth floor. He sets the cat down on the metal-slat landing to free a hand and slide up an apartment window. As he does so the cat makes to bolt. Llewyn corrals it, hugs it while he finishes getting the window up, and eases inside.

Before setting the cat down Llewyn closes the window behind him, then goes to the window next to it, which is cracked open, and closes that.

He sets down the cat.

A MINUTE LATER

Llewyn has the door to the refrigerator open and is angling his head to look inside.

SAUCER SET ON FLOOR

Llewyn's hand enters to pour some milk. The cat scurries in to lap at the milk. We hear the refrigerator door being opened and closed, off, and then receding footsteps followed by the heavy apartment door being opened and slammed shut.

INT. LEGACY RECORDS STAIRWAY

Llewyn ascends the dingy stairway of the kind of office building that would have cage elevators that might or might not work.

MEL'S OUTER OFFICE

Small, seedy. Musician photos on the wall suggest the business is music-related. Each posing musician has an arm around the same small stout middle-aged man. Some of the pictures are autographed, with sentiments to "Mel."

A pebbled-glass door standing ajar shows an inner office where the short, middle-aged Mel of the pictures sits behind a desk. His chin rests squarely on the desktop. His shoulders are slumped down behind the desk.

We see effort in his body as we hear something being dragged along the floor.

Mel relaxes and rolls his castored chair back. He stoops out of the chair and rises hoisting a filebox he has just pulled from under the desk. He drops it on the desktop and starts leafing through.

Llewyn is entering.

                    LLEWYN
How we doin?

                     MEL
We're doin great!

LLEWYN

Really? New record's doing well?

Mel is instantly sad.

MEL

Oh – how *we* doin. Not so hot, I gotta be honest. (*Projects.*)
Ginny, where's Cincinnati?

Her voice projects, like his, on the back and forth:

GINNY'S VOICE

. . . What?

MEL

Cincinnati. It's not in here.

GINNY'S VOICE

It should be in there.

MEL

It's not in here. I'm tellin ya.

GINNY'S VOICE

. . . Cincinnati?

Mel is still rummaging.

MEL

. . . Yeah.

GINNY'S VOICE

. . . I got it.

MEL

What?

GINNY'S VOICE

I got it.

MEL

Is it . . .

GINNY'S VOICE

What?

MEL

You got Cincinnati?

GINNY'S VOICE

Yeah. You want it?

MEL

. . . Could I have it?

GINNY'S VOICE

Should I bring it in?

MEL

Yeah.

Llewyn tries to reclaim the floor:

LLEWYN

Do you owe me anything? You have to owe me *some*thing.

MEL
(*sad shake of head*)

I wish.

Ginny enters with a file that Mel examines. She leaves.

. . . People need time, you know. Buy you as a solo act. Even *know* you're a solo act . . . (*Shaking his head at the file.*) Cincinnati is *not* good.

GINNY'S VOICE

That's it, right?

MEL
(*sad*)

Yeah, this is it. God help me.

LLEWYN

Nobody knew us when we were a duo. It's not like me and Mike were ever a big act. It's not a big reeducation. For the public. Mel. *Mel.*

Mel is roused from the file.

MEL

Yeah. Yeah. How ya doin?

24

LLEWYN
Mel, there was no advance on my solo record, there's gotta
be *some* royalty. Fucking Christ's sake, it's cold out, I don't
even have a winter coat.

                    MEL
Jesus Christ! Ya kiddin me!

He drops the file, shocked.

He rounds the desk and leaves the office.

Llewyn looks around, puzzled.

*Through the open door we see a wedge of the outer office. There is a
coat rack. Mel's hand enters to pluck a coat from it.*

The hand disappears and after a moment Mel reenters with the coat.

                    MEL
Take this, kid.

                    LLEWYN
Mel – no.

                    MEL
I insist! I insist!

                              LLEWYN
I don't want your fuckin coat! What'll you wear?

                                MEL
Kid – I'll get by.

                              LLEWYN
It won't even fit me! This is bullshit, Mel! This is just a big
fat fucking bluff!

                                MEL
BLUFF! Kid, what, what do you – Bluff! I offer you this!?
Get the fuck out of my office!

                              LLEWYN
All right. Thanks for the coat.

                                MEL
What? All right, wait, shit – Lemme give ya forty dollahs.

FOYER – BUILDING DIRECTORY – DAY

A finger enters to buzz BERKEY.

The door buzzes and clicks off its latch.

Llewyn pushes through it.

FIRST FLOOR

Nunzio is leaning out of his apartment door.

                              NUNZIO
     They home.

                              LLEWYN
     Yeah.

He starts up the stairs.

STAIRWELL

High, looking down.

We hear Llewyn panting as we see his hand sliding up the bannister.

                                26

Llewyn arrives at the apartment door and enters.

BERKEY APARTMENT

It is swung open by Jean, a young woman.

> JEAN

Explain the cat.

Beyond her, in the apartment's main room, a young man in camo fatigues and boots sits on a rocker, stroking the cat now in his lap. The young man's buzz cut shows off a high forehead.

> LLEWYN

It's the Gorfeins'. Sorry. I crashed there last night –

> YOUNG MAN

What's its name?

> LLEWYN

I don't know. He snuck out the door when –

> JEAN

Do you think you're staying here tonight?

> LLEWYN

Hoping to. Jim around?

> YOUNG MAN

It's a lovely cat.

> JEAN

Jim's not here. We told Troy he could crash here.

> YOUNG MAN

Troy Nelson. How are you?

> LLEWYN

Yeah, hey. Llewyn Davis.

> TROY

Oh – hello! I've heard your music – and heard many nice things *about* you. From Jim and Jean, and from others.

LLEWYN

You have not heard one nice thing about me from Jean.
Ever. Have you, Troy?

JEAN

You tell the Gorfeins you'll take care of their cat, and then
bring him here for us to take care of?

TROY

I've heard nice things from Jim and Jean. And others.

LLEWYN

I *didn't* – it just *happened* –

TROY

It's a peaceful cat. Very contented.

LLEWYN

So I can't stay here tonight.

JEAN

Look. We told Troy he could stay. We don't keep the couch
free on the chance you'll show up.

TROY

If this is awkward, I could hitch back to Fort Dix, after I
perform tonight.

JEAN

Don't be silly. We offered you the couch.

LLEWYN

You're gigging somewhere?

JEAN

Troy is playing at the Gaslight tonight. We're meeting Jim
there.

TROY

Well, I could sleep on the floor, here. Llewyn could have
the couch. I'm certainly not a man of comforts. Alternately
– I could hitch back to Fort Dix after the show.

*Jean scribbles furiously on a page of a spiral notebook. As she rips the
page out and hands it to Llewyn:*

JEAN

Llewyn can sleep on the floor. With his cat.

LLEWYN

It's the Gorfeins' cat.

He looks at the paper:

I'm pregnant.

He looks up at Jean.

. . . What the *fuck*!

TROY

Well, I don't want to put anyone out.

THE GASLIGHT

Onstage, now wearing slacks and sweater, Troy performs "The Last Thing on My Mind."

THE LAST THING ON MY MIND

It's a lesson too late for the learnin'
Made of sand, made of sand
In the wink of an eye my soul is turnin'
In your hand, in your hand

Are you going away with no word of farewell
Will there be not a trace left behind
Well, I could have loved you better
I didn't mean to be unkind
You know that was the last thing on my mind

You've got reasons a-plenty for goin'
This I know, this I know
For the weeds have been steadily growin'
Please don't go, please don't go

As I lie in my bed in the mornin'
Without you, without you
Each song in my breast dies a-bornin'
Without you, without you

In the audience, Llewyn sits near Jean, one empty seat between, both of them gazing up at the performance.

Hands enter from behind Llewyn to grab his shoulders and squeeze. The person – a young man – drops into the empty seat.

JIM

Hey Llewyn! Good to see you, man!

LLEWYN

Hey.

Llewyn smiles and is immediately uncertain whether to look as Jim leans away to give Jean a kiss.

Jim looks up at the performance.

At length, sotto voce, eyes still directed up at the stage:

LLEWYN

. . . What do you think?

JIM
(also looking up)

What?

LLEWYN

Him. Troy.

Jim shakes his head admiringly.

JIM

Wonderful performer.

LLEWYN

Is he?

JIM

Wonderful.

LLEWYN

Does he have . . . higher function?

VOICE

Shhh!

Llewyn looks around for the shusher, then leans in closer to Jim.

LLEWYN

Look Jim, I didn't want to mention this in front of Jean,
you know how she gets.

JIM

What do you mean?

LLEWYN

You know, just – I need a little money. I can pay you back
soon. That, and the last loan. There's a girl I know who's in
trouble. Needs to get fixed.

JIM

Not again.

The song is ending. Healthy applause. Llewyn leans in closer.

LLEWYN

Different girl. Don't tell Jean.

JIM

I can't get it without Jean knowing. It's okay, she'll be okay
with it.

LLEWYN

No no no, that's okay, I, uh, I can find it somewhere else.

Onstage:

TROY

Thank you very much. Thank you. There's someone special
in the audience tonight, who'll maybe get up and help me
out here if you give a round of applause . . .

Llewyn rolls his eyes.

LLEWYN

I don't have my guitar.

TROY

I know that you folks know'm and love'm, ladies and
gentlemen – Jim and Jean!

LLEWYN

Uh. Yeah.

He applauds with the crowd as Jim and Jean take the stage.

Three guitars and three voices: they perform "Five Hundred Miles."

FIVE HUNDRED MILES

If you miss the train I'm on, you will know that I am gone
You can hear the whistle blow a hundred miles
A hundred miles, a hundred miles
A hundred miles, a hundred miles
You can hear the whistle blow a hundred miles

Lord I'm one, Lord I'm two, Lord I'm three, Lord I'm four
Lord I'm five hundred miles away from home
Away from home, away from home
Away from home, away from home
Lord I'm five hundred miles away from home

Not a shirt on my back, not a penny to my name
Lord I can't go back home this a-way
This a-way, this a-way, this a-way, this a-way
Lord I can't go back home this a-way

Jean swivels at the mike she shares with Jim, giving the crowd eye contact. When her look crosses Llewyn it darkens.

He gives her a 'What-did-I-do?'

Her look moves on.

Pappi Corsicatto plops himself into the empty chair next to Llewyn.

PAPPI

Boy *they're* not bad.

LLEWYN

Uh-huh.

Staring beat. Then:

PAPPI

That Jean, I'd like to fuck her.

LLEWYN

. . . Yeah. I guess.

36

BERKEY APARTMENT

Early morning, Jim and Jean's apartment. The cat sits on the windowsill, gazing out at rooftops and water towers.

The clinking of a spoon. The cat looks around.

Troy Nelson sits in a low rocker, knees sticking up, once again in his fatigues and boots, spooning cereal from a bowl. In the background, the cat leaps down from the sill.

Llewyn, who has been sleeping on the floor, stirs.

> TROY
>
> Sorry. Early. Tried not to wake anyone.

> LLEWYN
>
> 'S okay.

> TROY
>
> Morning mess.

> LLEWYN
>
> Uh-huh.

Another clink; the crunch of corn flakes between teeth.

And another.

Troy sets his spoon down and looks at the bowl for a beat. Then he raises it with both hands and drains the milk from it. He clears his throat.

> TROY
>
> Well. That was very good.

Llewyn, resting on his side, props his head on a fist and stares.

> LLEWYN
>
> Well . . . What's next?

> TROY
>
> Whaddya mean?

> LLEWYN
>
> Do you . . . plug yourself in somewhere?

Troy blinks at him.

TROY
No.

His look holds for a beat, then wanders around the apartment. When it reaches Llewyn again he sighs, then slaps his belly.

Well. Report for duty. Back to Fort Dix.

LLEWYN
They making you a killing machine?

TROY
Oh, no – heh-heh! No, it's probably different from what you imagine. There's the discipline, which is what you're referring to. I thrive on that. The weaponry is – well, it's part of the job.

LLEWYN
Uh-huh.

He gets up, starts pushing his few effects into a bag.

TROY
Armaments are not my thing. I don't even approve of war toys.

LLEWYN
Is it a career?

TROY
No, no. I get out in a few months. Bud Grossman has expressed interest in representing me.

This gets Llewyn's attention.

LLEWYN
Bud Grossman. What's he like?

TROY
Mr. Grossman is a wonderful man. He's been very supportive. I played at his club in Chicago on my last furlough, right after I got back from Germany.

Llewyn swings his feet out and puts his pants on.

LLEWYN

You meet Elvis?

TROY

No. Everyone asks that. I did not meet Private Presley.

He has finished packing. Llewyn puts a cigarette in his mouth and pats himself down for matches.

LLEWYN

So you played at the Gate of Horn.

TROY

Yes. Mr. Grossman liked what he saw, I guess. He thinks I can have a career.

LLEWYN

Uh-huh.

He pushes the window open a foot and reclines on the couch, head towards window, to smoke.

Troy pauses with his kit at the door. Near the bedroom, he keeps his voice low:

TROY

. . . Thank Jim and Jean for me. Don't want to wake them.

LLEWYN

Will do.

TROY

Good meeting you.

LLEWYN

You too.

Troy goes through the door and eases it shut behind him.

Llewyn draws on the cigarette, angles the exhale towards the window, then looks back into the room.

The cat walks toward him, tail up, purring.

What's your name, again?

The cat leaps onto the sill and is out the window.

. . . Fuck!

He lunges for it, sticking an arm through the window over the fire escape – but is not even close.

He sticks his head out the window.

His point-of-view down: the cat pat-pat-pats away down the fire escape, toward the alley below, each step on the metal stairs giving the faintest clung.

LLEWYN

Fuck!

Llewyn draws his head back in, banging the back of it on the window sash, and bolts for the apartment door and through it, letting it close behind him with a SLAM.

STAIRWAY

He passes a surprised Troy Nelson one flight down.

LLEWYN

Cat!

EXT. TENEMENT

Llewyn bangs out the front door and sprints several feet to the alley mouth and into the alley.

ALLEY

No cat in sight. Llewyn walks down the alley in his T-shirt, hugging himself against the cold, looking from side to side.

LLEWYN

Cat . . . kitty . . . kitty . . . Fuck.

Nothing moving anywhere.

. . . Fuck.

Llewyn retraces his steps back up the alley. He emerges and looks one way down the street.

Early-morning empty. A couple of cars cross a block away.

He looks the other way.

Just as empty, except for one receding figure, already small: a camo-clad soldier with a guitar case in hand and a duffel bag on his shoulder.

BERKEY APARTMENT

Jean, in a nightie, opens the door to Llewyn.

> JEAN
> (*hissing*)
> Thanks for keeping quiet, asshole.

> LLEWYN
> I'm freezing! Can we talk?

> JEAN
> Not here! Fuck you!

> LLEWYN
> Well – I'm sorry, which? Out, or fuck you? Let's go out.
> Can I borrow Jim's coat?

> JEAN
> Fuck you!

WASHINGTON SQUARE

They walk along Washington Square North, Llewyn in the borrowed coat.

> JEAN
> I don't know!

> LLEWYN
> You don't know if it's mine.

> JEAN
> No! How would I know?

> LLEWYN
> So it could be Jim's.

JEAN

Yes! Asshole!

LLEWYN

But you don't want it either way. To be clear.

JEAN

To be clear, asshole, you fucking asshole, I want very much to have it if it's Jim's. That's what I *want*. But since I don't know, you not only fucked things up by fucking me and *maybe* making me pregnant, but even if it's *not* yours, I can't *know* that, so I have to get rid of what might be a perfectly fine baby. A baby I want. Because everything you touch turns to shit. Like King Midas's idiot brother.

LLEWYN

Well. Okay. I see.

JEAN

You know a doctor, right?

LLEWYN

Yes.

JEAN

From when – whatever – Diane.

LLEWYN

Yes.

JEAN

And you'll pay for it.

LLEWYN

Yes.

JEAN

Don't tell Jim. Obviously.

A silent beat of walking.

. . . I should have had you wear double condoms. Well – we shouldn't have done it in the first place. But if you ever do it again, which as a favor to women everywhere you should not, but if you do, you should be wearing condom on

44

condom. And then wrap it in electrical tape. You should just walk around always, inside a great big condom. Because you are shit.

LLEWYN

Okay.

JEAN

You should not be in contact with any living thing. Being shit.

Walking beat.

LLEWYN

. . . You know the expression, It takes two to tango –

JEAN

Oh, fuck you.

Walking beat.

LLEWYN

I could say, we should talk about this when you're less angry, but that would be . . . that would be . . . When would that be –

JEAN

Fuck you.

They walk for a beat.

. . . I miss Mike.

LLEWYN

Could I ask you for a favor?

JEAN

You're joking.

LLEWYN

Not for me, it's for the Gorfeins. Their cat got out – could you leave the fire-escape window open?

She stares at him.

JEAN

It's winter.

                    LLEWYN
Just enough for the cat? To squeeze back in? It could come
back.

                    JEAN
Come back? To our apartment? It was there like six hours!
Why would it come back there?

For the first time in the conversation Llewyn is exercised.

                    LLEWYN
I don't know, I'm not a fucking cat! Think about it, I lost
their fucking cat! I feel bad about it!

                    JEAN
That's what you feel bad about?

SUBWAY CAR

*Train rumble bangs in at the cut. We are close on Llewyn, body
joggling with the motion of the train. The window behind his head is,
in the black of the train tunnel, a dull mirror of the car.*

Long hold.

*The window pops into brightness as the train emerges onto a bridge
approach, giving us a brief view down the East River.*

QUEENS STREET

Llewyn is a small figure receding down a quiet residential street.

QUEENS STOOP

Llewyn sits on a stoop reading a newspaper, elbows on knees.

At a sound, he looks up.

*A woman a little older than him is coming up the walk with a bag of
groceries. She is surprised to see him.*

                    WOMAN
Hello. Where's ya coat?

48

Llewyn stands, folding the newspaper.

> LLEWYN

Not that cold.

> WOMAN

Y'out a ya mind?

QUEENS KITCHEN

Llewyn sits at the table as the woman puts away groceries.

> WOMAN

So how's the music goin?

> LLEWYN

Oh, pretty good. Pretty good.

> WOMAN

Oh good. So you don't need to borrow money.

A beat as she continues to put things away.

> LLEWYN

Actually, I was wondering . . .

> WOMAN

Uh-huh?

> LLEWYN

Is it sold?

> WOMAN

The house?

> LLEWYN

Yeah.

> WOMAN

Yeah, uh-huh. I mean it's in escrow.

> LLEWYN

For what?

> WOMAN

Eleven-five, but – why? It's not our house.

49

                                LLEWYN
Not our *house*?

                                WOMAN
Well, yeah – Mom and Dad's house. Llewyn, it goes to his
upkeep.

                                LLEWYN
Right.

                                WOMAN
We don't get any.

Beat.

        . . . Good thing ya music's goin good.

Another beat.

        . . . I'm sorry.

                                LLEWYN
Yeah, well. What the fuck.

                                WOMAN
Llewyn.

                                LLEWYN
What?

                                WOMAN
The language.

                                LLEWYN
Oh – yeah. Sorry.

                                WOMAN
I am not one a' ya Greenwich Village friends.

                                LLEWYN
Okay, yeah.

She eyes him for a beat.

                                WOMAN
Still got ya seaman's papers?

LLEWYN

Yeah. Why?

WOMAN

If the music's not . . .

LLEWYN

What – quit?! Merchant marine again? Just . . . exist?

She laughs.

WOMAN

"Exist"? That's what we do outside of show business? It's
not so bad, existing.

LLEWYN

Like Dad?

WOMAN

Llewyn!

LLEWYN

What?

WOMAN

You say that about your own fatha!

LLEWYN

What?

WOMAN

That he "*exists*"!

LLEWYN

I didn't say – you said it! I – forget it.

WOMAN

That he "exists"! Like that?!

LLEWYN

Yeah yeah. Sorry.

WOMAN

. . . Seen him?

LLEWYN

Yeah. What? Should I?

WOMAN

You tell me. He's ya fatha.

LLEWYN

Yeah, right. He sure is.

WOMAN
(*rising*)

I got – wait – I got – you got a minute?

LLEWYN

Well they, they want me back, rehearsals for the Sullivan show. And I got some autographs to sign. Champagne reception . . .

WOMAN
(*leaving*)

Don't go way.

He looks idly around.

Working-class kitchen. Oilcloth on the table. Some seafaring knick-knacks.

WOMAN
(*projected, from off*)

I cleaned it out, the house. There was some stuff. I put ya stuff in a box . . .

She reenters with an open box.

. . . What I thought ya might want.

She sets it on the table in front of him. He looks with no particular interest, flips through a couple of things, shrugs.

LLEWYN

I don't know, Joy, just, what would I . . . Just stick it out at the curb.

WOMAN

Llewyn! Are you kiddin? Lookit this. You know what this is?

She is pulling out an EP-sized record in a plain white sleeve.

. . . This is when you recorded "Shoals of Herring" for Mom and Dad!

He looks at her, shrugs a "So-what?"

. . . You're whateva, you're like eight years old! It's so cute!

LLEWYN

Well, see, Joy, in the entertainment business you're never supposed to let your practice shit out. Ruins the mystique.

She is disappointed that he won't share her enthusiasm.

JOY

I'm sorry, I don't know a lot about the entertainment business.

LLEWYN

Yeah. Well. Don't be sorry.

SUBWAY PLATFORM

A Queens open-air station. Llewyn is on a pay phone.

LLEWYN

No no no, I'll bring the cat up, it's fine, I just, not today as it turns out, I can't bring her today –

VOICE

He.

LLEWYN

– He. He's hanging out at Jim and Jean's, he likes it there, he's fine, believe me.

VOICE

I'll run down and pick him up, I don't want to –

LLEWYN

No no no, they're never home, anyway I couldn't ask you to do that, all the way down to the Village, I'll bring her up tomorrow. Him.

VOICE

Okay. Okay. And remember to call Jim. He said it was urgent.

                                    LLEWYN
            Yeah, I doubt if it's urgent but yeah, I'll call him, thanks.

                                    VOICE
            No, he said it's urgent. A session this afternoon at
            Columbia, somebody got sick, dropped out – he thought
            you'd like the work –

*Llewyn projects over the roar of an approaching train which, from our
perspective, buries the voice at the other end.*

                                    LLEWYN
            What? WHAT? Do I need my guitar? . . . DID HE SAY
            DO I NEED MY GUITAR? . . . NO!?

The approaching train roars into frame.

COLUMBIA RECORDS

*The Columbia Records logo is etched into the glass double-doors
leading to reception.*

Llewyn bangs through.

INSIDE

He goes up to the receptionist.

                                    LLEWYN
            I'm here for Mr. Cromartie's session? Llewyn Davis?

                                    RECEPTIONIST
            Have a seat, I'll let him know you're here.

SEATING AREA

Minutes later.

Llewyn sits waiting, on furniture more expensive than he is used to.

Very, very quiet.

He looks around.

Gold records on the wall, tastefully framed.

Black-and-white photographs, nicely lit, of performers, in the studio. Different genres are represented – Dizzy Gillespie, Johnny Mathis, a young Leonard Bernstein.

The muted click of a door latch draws Llewyn's attention.

Ambling down the hall, hands dug into pockets, is a distinguished, Waspy gentleman in tweeds. Llewyn jumps to his feet.

CROMARTIE

Llewyn?

LLEWYN

Mr. Cromartie, an honor to meet you.

CROMARTIE

Where's your guitar?

STUDIO

A nice but not especially large studio. Jim is walking Llewyn in, beaming, arm around his shoulder.

JIM

You'll play a Gibson, right?

LLEWYN

Yours? Sure. You're playing –

JIM

The D-15. You know Al?

Another young man, with guitar, is at one of the three stools ranged around a microphone.

LLEWYN

Hey man.

VOICE
(*through the talk-back*)

Read a chart, Llewyn?

It is Cromartie who, in the control room, stands behind the board.

LLEWYN

I . . . I . . . can stare at a chart and fake it, sir.

Mutely, behind the glass, Cromartie laughs. We get the tail of the laugh as he punches in:

>   CROMARTIE
> Jim and Al will teach it to you. Take your time. We're here
> to have fun.

>   LLEWYN
> Okay. (*To Jim.*) So . . . We're the, the what? The John Glenn
> Singers?

He looks up.

His point-of-view: a high ceiling. Hanging sound reflectors of blond wood.

>   CROMARTIE'S VOICE
> It's not the most serious music we've recorded here.

>   JIM
>   (*explanatory*)
> It's a thing.

MANY MINUTES LATER

The three men are setting themselves at the microphone.

>   LLEWYN
> So I'm going down on "capsule," I'm doing this . . .

He demonstrates on guitar.

>   AL
> Yeah, I'm taking the high . . .

They run through a couple of phrases, voice and guitar, not full volume.

>   LLEWYN
> Okay. Okay. (*Low.*) I'm happy for the gig, but . . . who *wrote*
> this?

Jim looks uncomfortable.

                              JIM
       I did.

                          CROMARTIE
                       (*through talk-back*)
       Okay?

Some last-minute arranging of weight on stools. Throat clears.

                              JIM
       So, okay.

                          CROMARTIE
       Good?

                              AL
       Okay.

                          CROMARTIE
       One second.

Waiting beat.

Muted back-and-forth in the control room between Cromartie and the engineer. Cromartie laughs silently. Engineer, smiling, nods. Engineeer checks something. Cromartie gets serious, leans forward for the talk-back button:

                          CROMARTIE
       Okay . . . "Please, Mr. Kennedy" take one. Sound of a
       blast-off and . . . we're rolling.

Al and Llewyn look to Jim who nods in time, whispering a count-off:

                              JIM
       . . . Two, three, four . . .

And they perform the song.

                     PLEASE, MR. KENNEDY

       Ten, nine, eight, seven, six, five, four, three, two . . .
       One second, please

       Please, Mr. Kennedy
       I don't wanna go
       Please don't shoot me into outer space

I sweat when they stuff me into pressure suits
Bubble helmet, Flash Gordon boots
No air up there in gravity zero
I need to breathe, don't need to be a hero
And are you reading me loud and clear? Oh!

I'm six-foot-two, and so perhaps you'll
Tell me how to fit into a five-foot capsule
I won't be known as man of the century
If I'm blubbering upon reentry

Got a red-blooded wife with a healthy libido
You'll lose her vote if you make her a widow
And who'll play catch out in the back with our kid? Oh!

CORNER OF THE STUDIO

Some time later.

Llewyn sits on a folding chair, one of several along one wall, near a table on which sit a coffee percolator and some cups and other paraphernalia. Mike stands are ranged nearby.

Jim and Al are shrugging into coats. Another man, in shirtsleeves and tie, stands over Llewyn who has a pen and a clipboard holding papers. As he squints at the top sheet, Llewyn addresses Jim:

LLEWYN
No, thank *you*, I appreciate it. I needed this. As you know.

JIM
Don't thank me, thank Richie Sheridan. Puked his way out of the John Glenn Singers.

LLEWYN
Tough luck. We'll be touring, right?

Al laughs.

AL
Touring my ass.

LLEWYN
I'll get my vaccinations. (*To shirtsleeved man as he continues to squint at papers.*) Where?

59

                              MAN
You *are* AF of M right?

                            LLEWYN
Yeah.

                              MAN
Sign there and there. You don't have a label?

                            LLEWYN
I do – Legacy.

                              MAN
You're exclusive to Mel? I'll need a permission. He'll give
you one.

                            LLEWYN
But it'll take, shit . . . I need the money *now*.

The man shrugs.

                              MAN
You wanna just be an independent contractor, accounting'll
give you a check today. Bill us for services, $200. It's more
than the session fee 'cause you don't get royalties.

                            LLEWYN
Okay. And I can cash it?

                              MAN
Sure, right around the corner. But you don't go on the
session sheet then, no royalties.

                            LLEWYN
That's fine. That's okay . . .

As he signs:

      . . . Where do you live, Al?

                              AL
Downing Street.

                            LLEWYN
Nice place?

AL

Dump.

                    LLEWYN

Uh-huh. Got a couch?

LEGACY RECORDS

The seedy office where earlier we met Mel Novikoff.

We hear the clack of a typewriter as we push in. Now, though, the inside doorway to Mel's office stands ajar, exposing desk and empty chair and late sun.

Llewyn looks over at Ginny, typing something.

                    LLEWYN

Where's Mel?

Ginny, eyes on her work, replies absently while still typing:

                    GINNY

Mel, is at . . . a funeral.

                    LLEWYN

Boy, that man goes to a lot of funerals.

                    GINNY

He likes people.

                    LLEWYN

Fewer and fewer!

                    GINNY

This is family. His nephew Georgie is engaged to a girl whose mother just passed.

                    LLEWYN

I . . . don't know if that's family.

Ginny's eyes remain on her work.

                    GINNY

He likes funerals, I don't know what to tell you.

LLEWYN

I forgot to pick up my mail yesterday. So pissed at Mel.

GINNY

Ya didn't forget to pick up your mail.

LLEWYN

Yes I did.

GINNY

You don't have any mail.

LLEWYN

Oh.

(*beat*)

Shit. Nothing?

(*she types on; he is hesitant*)

. . . I didn't get anything from Bud Grossman? In Chicago?

GINNY

You were supposed to get something from Bud Grossman?

LLEWYN

I had Mel send him my solo record. When it came out. Whenever, more than a month ago.

GINNY

Oh!

She stops typing and rises, giving Llewyn momentary hope.

. . . No, you didn't get anything, but we were making space in the stock room and dumped the rest of the old record. All the remainduhs. Yours and Mikey's . . .

She hoists a box from behind the counter.

. . . Mel set one box aside, thought you might want to keep some copies.

Llewyn pulls a copy from the box, shaking his head, and looks at the cover.

The artists are Timlin and Davis, Llewyn himself recognizable though clean-shaven, looking only a little younger, on a stool with a guitar, mouth frozen mid-song. Standing behind him is, presumably, Mike Timlin, transported by the music, joyously vocalizing to the heavens with his body tensed and his hands turned up. The name of the record is, "If We Had Wings!"

LLEWYN

Whuh . . . I . . . (*Shrugs.*) What'm I gonna do with 'em?

Ginny resumes typing.

GINNY

Should I throw 'em out?

LEGACY RECORDS BUILDING HALLWAY

"Dink's Song" plays. Llewyn walks the broad dingy hallway, the box of records hugged against his stomach.

LEGACY RECORDS BUILDING — STAIRWAY

Llewyn descends encumbered with records.

MIDTOWN STREET

The song continues to play as Llewyn walks the slushy street.

VILLAGE STREET

More walking, Llewyn sweating, box held awkwardly out before his stomach.

AL CODY'S VESTIBULE

The box is body-pressed against the vestibule wall and Llewyn's freed hand goes to the directory. It finds CODY 6A, *and buzzes.*

AL CODY'S STAIRWELL

We are looking down six flights' worth of stairwell. We catch glimpses of Llewyn ascending, midway up, some of his shoulder and his arm pressing box to stomach swinging into view with each laborious footfall.

AL CODY'S SIXTH-FLOOR HALLWAY

A spent Llewyn drops the box to the floor and leans against the door jamb of 6A and knocks, panting.

We jump in as Al, from the recording session, opens the door.

> AL
> Good, here's the key. I'm running out to Jersey to pick up my mother's car.

> LLEWYN
> (*heavy panting*)
> Okay.

AL CODY'S APARTMENT

Llewyn looks around the small studio, hands on hips.

He sits and bounces experimentally on the couch: how's this one? He swings his legs up and lies back to see if it affords full extension. Pretty close.

He rises, and bends down to shove his record box under Al's couch. It won't go under all the way; something is blocking.

Llewyn peeks, reaches under, pulls out an uncovered box similar to his, packed with LPs.

He pulls one out showing that the box contains copies of one record. Its title: "Another Point of View." The artist: Al Cody. The cover photograph of Al, whom we've only seen happy, has him looking rather pensive.

Llewyn gazes at the album.

BERKEY FOYER

Llewyn rings BERKEY 6C.

A beat.

> JEAN'S VOICE
>
> Yeah?

> LLEWYN
>
> It's me. Llewyn.

> JEAN'S VOICE
>
> *Yeah?*

> LLEWYN
>
> Can I come up?

> JEAN'S VOICE
>
> No.

> LLEWYN
>
> Well – okay. Well. Can I have my stuff?

A beat.

> JEAN
>
> . . . I'll bring it down. I'll meet you at the Reggio.

INT. CAFE REGGIO

Jean sits into close shot. We are in a dark Italian coffee shop.

> JEAN
>
> Who won the lottery tonight?

> LLEWYN
>
> Huh? Oh. I'm staying at Al Cody's. So. When do you want to do this thing?

> JEAN
>
> The abortion? The sooner the better. Tomorrow if I can. Jim won't be around, I won't have to make up a story where I'm going.

> LLEWYN
>
> Okay, I'll see if the guy can do it then.

> JEAN
>
> The *guy*? I hope he's a doctor.

LLEWYN

Yeah yeah, he's a doctor.

JEAN

You got the money?

LLEWYN

Yeah, I got the money – don't worry.

JEAN

With you I worry.

LLEWYN

Well, you shouldn't.

JEAN

Yes, I should. God knows *you* never do. You just let other people. Like your method of birth control.

LLEWYN

Please don't start with the double-condoms again.

JEAN

Do you ever think about the future at all?

LLEWYN

The future? You mean like, flying cars? Hotels on the moon? Tang?

JEAN

And this is why you're fucked.

LLEWYN

No, it's why *you're* fucked. Trying to blueprint a future. Move to the suburbs. With Jim. Have kids.

JEAN

That's bad?

LLEWYN

If that's what music is, for you, a way to get to that place, then yes – it's a little careerist. A little square. And a little sad.

JEAN

I'm sad! *You're* the one who's not getting anywhere! You
don't even *want* to get anywhere! Me and Jim *try*!

Llewyn gropes:

LLEWYN

I do wanna . . . I wanna –

JEAN

We *try*! You sleep on the *couch*!

LLEWYN

Bad thing to throw in my face, man!

JEAN

You don't wanna go anywhere, and that's why all the *same
shit* is going to keep happening to you. Because you *want*
it to.

LLEWYN

Is that why?

JEAN

And also because – you're an *asshole*! Let's not forget *that*!
Who sleeps with other people's *women*!

LLEWYN

Well, you're being pretty kind to yourself now, aren't you!

JEAN

Whose couch are you on *tonight*?

LLEWYN

I told you, Al Cody's.

He is tensing, rising, looking out the window.

. . . You don't listen, you just, spout vitriol . . .

*Jean looks at him, puzzled by the trance he has entered. His eyes
widen further.*

. . . Keep an eye on my shit!

He bolts.

STREET

Llewyn pounds down the sidewalk, missing most – but bumping some – of the pedestrians.

> LLEWYN
> HEY!

A couple of people glance around; none of them are his focus. He pounds along.

> . . . HEY!

As he nears the object of his pursuit his eyeline drops.

> . . . Hey! Hey! Hey!

He is hastily crouch-walking now and he reaches forward and scoops –

The Gorfeins' cat, which twists and struggles, but only a little, as Llewyn tucks him against his chest.

BACK IN CAFE REGGIO

Llewyn enters with the cat.

> LLEWYN
> God damn. I am one lucky bastard. Thank you for suggesting this place.

He glances furtively around, then takes his coffee cup off its saucer and pours cream into it from the silver creamer. He sets the cat on the table to feed.

> . . . Thing can't have eaten since yesterday, it's a damn housecat.

Jean watches the cat lap milk. Llewyn pets it and it pushes back against his hand, purring as it continues to lap milk.

> . . . Do you know his name? I can't remember its name.

> JEAN
> I don't know its name. I don't hang out with the Gorfeins.

> LLEWYN
> Jesus. Thank God. Good kitty. Well – where were we?

All the acrimony is spent. The exchange is matter-of-fact:

> JEAN
>
> You were calling me a careerist. And I was calling you a loser.

> LLEWYN
>
> Right. Well. Those are your categories.

> JEAN
>
> No – those are your categories.

> LLEWYN
>
> Ya know, in my experience the world is divided into two kinds of people: Those who divide the world into two categories –

> JEAN
>
> – and losers?

EXTERIOR AL CODY'S BUILDING / STREET

As Llewyn walks up, someone is pulling something out of the back seat of a car parked just in front of the building.

The person, emerging with a box, is Al Cody.

> AL
>
> Oh – hey man. Can you bring this up for me? – This ain't a spot. Just brought some stuff from home.

> LLEWYN
>
> Yeah, sure.

Already holding his own guitar and wearing shoulder sack, Llewyn takes the cardboard box somewhat awkwardly. It holds odds and ends, with a short stack of mail on top.

Al is retreating to the car, a big Plymouth Belvedere.

> AL
>
> Hey, you don't need to crash more than a couple days, do you? My girlfriend's coming down from Boston Tuesday.

> LLEWYN
>
> Oh. Yeah, no, that's fine, okay. Thanks.

Al hesitates in the open car door, looking at Llewyn over the roof.

> AL
>
> Don't wanna go to Chicago, do you?

> LLEWYN
>
> Why would I want to go to Chicago?

> AL
>
> Yeah, right. My car is going to Chicago Tuesday.

> LLEWYN
>
> Uh-huh.

> AL
>
> Friend of mine is driving someone to a gig. They're looking for someone to help pay for gas.

> LLEWYN
>
> I . . . prefer New York. Who's Arthur Milgrum?

Llewyn has been moved to ask by the mail he is looking at, lying atop the other effects in the box.

> AL
>
> Oh – that's me. Gonna change it legally, at some point.

AL CODY'S STAIRWELL

Llewyn ascending, only partly visible, halfway up, laboring under his load.

AL CODY'S APARTMENT

A saucer is placed on the floor in close shot, milk is poured, and the cat runs purring into frame.

DR. MARCUS RUVKUN'S WAITING ROOM

A door opens and a uniformed nurse emerges from an inner office and steps into the foreground.

> NURSE
>
> Mr. Davis?

The reverse shows Llewyn incongruously sitting among pregnant women. He rises.

DR. MARCUS RUVKUN'S CONSULTATION ROOM

Llewyn is now seated across a desk from the doctor, Marcus Ruvkun.

Llewyn is shaking his head.

> LLEWYN
>
> No no, she won't want me with her.

> MARCUS
>
> Okay, well, she should have a friend though, someone who can help her home.

> LLEWYN
>
> Okay, I'll tell her.

> MARCUS
>
> It'll have to be on a Saturday, I can do it this Saturday.

> LLEWYN
>
> Okay. I'll pay you now since I won't see you. Cash I, uh –

He is reaching into a pocket.

> MARCUS
>
> No no! No charge.

Llewyn is flummoxed.

> LLEWYN
>
> . . . What?

> MARCUS
>
> You know, from last time.

> LLEWYN
>
> . . . From last time? You mean Diane?

> MARCUS
>
> Yeah. I didn't have a number, or an address for you. Where do you live, anyway?

LLEWYN

Wait, what?

MARCUS

I didn't have a –

LLEWYN

Why is there no charge this time?

MARCUS

Huh?

LLEWYN

Why –

MARCUS

Well, *you* know.

Awkward beat.

LLEWYN

Well – no, I *don't* know, man. You working pro-bono now?

MARCUS

Well, no, since it didn't happen last time.

Longer beat.

LLEWYN

What didn't happen?

Marcus blinks.

MARCUS

Diane didn't tell you? (*Responds to Llewyn's look.*) Diane did not terminate the pregnancy. She came in to tell me she'd decided to . . . go to . . . term. (*Another beat.*) She didn't tell you?

LLEWYN

Uh . . . no.

MARCUS

She . . . jeez. She asked me to refer her to a doctor in Akron.

                         LLEWYN
In Akron . . .

                         MARCUS
To deliver the, uh . . .

                         LLEWYN
The – the . . . Uh-huh. (*A beat.*) I knew she was going to
Akron. She's from Akron.

                         MARCUS
Yes. I'm sorry, I thought –

                         LLEWYN
Her parents are in Akron.

                         MARCUS
Uh-huh.

                         LLEWYN
. . . The kid'd be about two now?

                         MARCUS
Yeah, I guess . . . Yes . . . I'm sorry. I didn't know how to
get the money back to you. I never see you at the hoots
anymore.

SUBWAY CAR

*Llewyn sits in the middling-crowded car, cat hugged to his chest,
staring vacantly down, mentally chewing, body moving with the
motion of the car. At length he shrugs away his thought, whatever
it was, and his look drifts.*

It catches on something.

*A strap-hanging businessman is looking at him. Is it the same one he
saw going downtown from the Gorfeins'?*

THE GORFEINS' ELEVATOR

*The same operator is holding the throttle down in the Gorfeins' elevator
looking suspiciously behind him as the floors slip by outside the gate.*

Llewyn is standing at the back of the cab holding the cat securely against his chest. We hear a fist rapping.

THE GORFEINS' APARTMENT

The door swings open to reveal a short, bespectacled middle-aged man in a cardigan.

> MITCH

There's the cat!

It spills out of Llewyn's arms and runs into the apartment. Mitch hugs Llewyn.

> . . . Home from the hill! Llewyn, welcome! Come on in, Lillian is in the kitchen making her famous moussaka!

> LLEWYN

Oh, that's okay, I can't barge in for dinner, I just wanted to –

Mitch pulls him into the apartment.

> MITCH

No, what're you talking about, one more person – moussaka?! C'mon . . . Do you know Marty Green and Janet Fung?

A Jewish-looking man and a Chinese woman nod and smile greeting.

> LLEWYN

Nice to meet you, Llewyn Davis.

> MARTY GREEN

Oh! Mitch and Lillian's folk song friend!

> MITCH

You crashing with us?

> LLEWYN

No no, I hadn't even planned on dinner –

> MITCH

Llewyn's not an Upper West Side guy. We only get to see him when he's . . .

LLEWYN

When I've rotated through my Village friends.

MITCH

We're the last resort. Marty is in my department – and Joe
is a musician, this is Joe Flom, he plays in Musica Anticha
with Lillian.

LLEWYN

Hey, how ya doing.

JOE

Nice to meet you.

LLEWYN

What's your instrument?

JOE

Well, anything with a keyboard, I play celeste and
harpsichord in MA. I'm a piano instructor most days.

LLEWYN

Bum a cigarette?

JOE

Sure.

MITCH

Glass of wine, Llewyn? Little dago red?

LLEWYN

Sure, I uh, I should've brought something.

MITCH

Don't be silly, you brought the cat.

LLEWYN

I took piano lessons when I was a kid, from Mrs. Sieglestein.
You don't know Mrs. Sieglestein, do ya? Very big calves,
orthopedic shoes? Lives in Far Rockaway? Upstairs from
the Kurlands?

JOE

Does she play early music?

LLEWYN

Harry James, on the radio. On piano she played mostly, what, we played, uh, "Drink to Me Only with Thine Eyes." I don't know. Sounded early.

JOE

Uh-huh.

LLEWYN

She was not a swinger.

JOE

Well – Harry James.

LLEWYN

Well, okay. Her playing though, pretty on the beat.

JOE

You still play piano?

LLEWYN

I'll sit down and fiddle with anything, but not really. Not so's it sounds pretty.

JOE

Well, with practice . . .

GORFEINS' DINING ROOM

Insert on a picture of a strange-looking two-year-old, half Asian, half something else.

At the cut the clink-clank of a dinner table, and Llewyn's voice:

LLEWYN

He's . . . he's adorable. How old is he?

Wider on the dinner table as he hands the picture back to Janet Fung.

JANET

Turned two in April. He's with my mother now.

MARTY

Grandmas come in handy.

LLEWYN

What's his name?

MARTY

Howie.

JANET

He already calls him Howie. *Howard.*

MARTY

Howie Greenfung.

LLEWYN

What, like, Green, Fung? Hyphenated?

MARTY

No no, one word. Greenfung.

JANET

Howard Greenfung.

LLEWYN

You're – kidding, right?

JANET
(*puzzled; ready to take offense*)

No.

MITCH
(*leaping in*)

Why don't you give us a song, Llewyn?

LLEWYN

Oh – no, I –

LILLIAN

Oh, please – he's very good. Joe should hear you.

MITCH

And Marty and Janet.

LILLIAN

Well of *course* Marty and Janet.

LLEWYN

No, they don't need to sit through –

Mitch rises.

MITCH

I'm getting my Kalamazoo. You get to play it if and only if you sing.

LLEWYN

Okay, yeah, I can tell, this is one of those things, I keep saying no you think I'm just asking you to beg more.

LILLIAN

That's right.

LLEWYN

You know, I'm not a trained poodle.

Mitch reenters with guitar case.

LILLIAN

I thought singing was a joyous expression of the soul.

LLEWYN

Boy. Nice instrument.

He takes it, runs a couple of licks.

. . . This is, this one's pretty early, Joe should like it.

Receptive chuckles from the little audience.

Llewyn starts playing, and singing, "Dink's Song."

The small group listens, genuinely taken with the performance.

As Llewyn begins the second verse, Lillian Gorfein eases in a high, sweet harmony.

Llewyn stops playing.

LLEWYN
(*sharply*)

What are you doing?

The spell is broken. The little audience is puzzled. Lillian is lost.

LILLIAN

. . . What?

LLEWYN

What is that? What're you doing?

LILLIAN

I –

LLEWYN

Don't do that.

LILLIAN

... It's ... it's Mike's part ...

LLEWYN

I know what it is. Don't do that. You know what?

He is more and more testy as he opens the guitar case and lays the guitar inside.

... This is bullshit. I don't do this. I do this for a *living*, you know? I'm a musician. I sing for a living. It's not a parlor game.

MITCH

Llewyn, please – that's unfair to Lillian –

LLEWYN

This is bullshit. I don't ask you over for dinner and then suggest you give us a lecture on the peoples of Meso-America or whatever your pre-Columbian shit is. This is my *job*. This is how I pay the fucking *rent*.

Lillian rises. She is choking up.

LILLIAN

Llewyn, that's not, this is not – this is a loving home!

LLEWYN

I'm a fucking professional. And you know what, *fuck* Mike's part.

LILLIAN

This is terrible. This is dreadful.

MITCH

It's okay, Lillian.

LILLIAN

I'm going – I'm going – I do not want to be in this room.

She leaves, weeping.

LLEWYN

Well, she doesn't have to leave. I'm leaving. Obviously.
Thank you for the moussaka. I'm sorry if I fucked up your
evening.

*Walla of protestation, calls for calm, from Mitch, Joe, Marty Green –
cut short by a scream.*

Everyone freezes, looking to where Lillian exited.

A still beat.

Lillian rushes in, holding the cat up, face-out, by its front paws.

LILLIAN

This is not our cat!

A staring beat. Mitch's mouth hangs open.

MITCH

. . . Oh my God!

LLEWYN

What? . . . Of *course* it's your cat.

MITCH

Oh my God, Llewyn!

LLEWYN

No, that's – that's your –

LILLIAN

It's not even a *male*!

Lillian shakes the cat, its jiggling body emphasizing her point

Where's its *scrotum*?!

LLEWYN

. . . I . . . It's –

83

Llewyn, WHERE'S ITS SCROTUM!

MITCH

Oh my God. Llewyn!

Black.

Fade in:

A point-of-view through a windshield, moving down a Village street. Slushy, grey, early morning. A figure is waiting at the curb, guitar case and small bag at his feet, holding a cat to his chest.

Cut outside as we pull up.

The car is a big four-door. The driver is an all-American young man, good-looking, although something not quite right about his face makes him less than a matinee idol. His blond hair is combed back in a pompadour. The stub of a cigarette hangs from his lip.

Llewyn looks in the back seat. A large man in a fedora is very still inside, asleep or passed out. Next to him are two canes with silver animal knobs.

The pompadoured driver, though he has stopped for Llewyn, seems to be ignoring him.

Llewyn opens the back door and stows the case upright, careful not to disturb the – sleeping? – fat man. He has a goatee and sunglasses. He has a feather in his broad-brimmed fedora and an animal fetish tie pin. His french cuffs are secured with bangles.

Llewyn gingerly shuts the door and climbs in front.

The driver puts the car in gear and starts driving.

Llewyn, somewhat bewildered, looks at the wordless driver – white T-shirt, leather jacket – staring out at the road. Llewyn looks back at the big man in the back seat, whose body now joggles with the motion of the car.

Llewyn turns back to the driver.

LLEWYN

Hello.

The driver's eyes stay on the road.

DRIVER

Yeah, heya.

LATER — IN COUNTRYSIDE

Llewyn is vacant, nodding, looking out.

Elaborate gagging and wake-snarfling noises from the back seat draw his attention.

The man in back stirs, smacks his lips, looks around.

He sees the guitar case.

ROLAND TURNER

What's this?

LLEWYN

My guitar.

ROLAND TURNER

Sure, move in, make yourself at home, don't mind me.

LLEWYN

He said the trunk was full.

Driving beat.

ROLAND TURNER

What're you, a flamenco dancer? What's your name? Pablo?

LLEWYN

Llewyn Davis.

ROLAND TURNER

I'm Roland Turner. This is my valet, Johnny Five.

Llewyn looks at Johnny Five.

Johnny Five is still unemotively focused on the road. The butt still burns on his lower lip, though it seems to be the same length.

Llewyn looks back at Roland Turner.

LLEWYN

Yeah, we met. I think.

Roland Turner is fully awake and has a lot to say.

ROLAND TURNER

And that was the last time I was in Murfreesboro. Gave me to understand I would not be welcomed back. I said, that's okay, brother, I might have managed on my own not to make it back to your little flyspeck horseshit town. What's the N stand for?

LLEWYN

. . . What?

ROLAND TURNER

What's the N stand for? Lou N. Davis?

LLEWYN

Llewyn. Llewyn. L-L-E-W-Y-N. It's Welsh.

ROLAND TURNER

Well it would have to be something, stupid fucking name like that. You don't look Welsh.

LLEWYN

My mother was Ital—

ROLAND TURNER

Here, this would interest you, Johnny and I were in Seattle, playing the High Spot – remember this, Johnny? – and I became indisposed after eating a toasted cheese sandwich. May well have been a rancid slice of bacon. Found myself purging from every orifice – one of them like a firehose – I said to the manager "What do you call that thing I just ate?" He said "Welsh rarebit." I said, "Okay, does everything from Wales make you shit yourself or just this piece of toast?" He said, and I'll never forget it because it almost made the experience worthwhile, he said, "Mr. Turner –" Holy Jesus what is that thing?

He has seen the cat, peeking over Llewyn's shoulder.

LLEWYN

My cat. Well not my cat, it's uh . . .

89

ROLAND TURNER

Grown man with a cat? Is it part of your act?

LLEWYN

No.

ROLAND TURNER

What'd you say you play? Flamenco?

LLEWYN

Folk songs.

ROLAND TURNER

Folk songs! I thought you said you were a musician. Folk singer with a cat. You queer?

LLEWYN

Ah – I – it's not my cat. I just didn't know what to do with it.

ROLAND TURNER

Oh yeah? So did you bring your dick along too? I'll tell you something about Welsh rarebit you probably didn't know, at least the way they make it at the the High Spot according to the manager, Dickie Wardlow – ever played for Dickie? Well no, you wouldn't've it's a music club, he said, I asked about the fucking toast he said –

Outside the window something attracts his attention.

Johnny, hold up, there's a Sinclair station. Your turn to pay for gas, Elwyn.

GAS STATION LOT

In the foreground Llewyn, back to us, leans against the car. Receding across the lot toward the station in the background is Roland Turner, elegantly dressed, herky-jerking away with his two canes.

MINUTES LATER

Llewyn comes out of the gas-station office with a soda.

Johnny Five is leaning against the building, one knee bent and foot planted against the brick. His thumbs are hooked in his pockets.

Llewyn looks at the empty car, looks at Johnny Five.

LLEWYN

He still in there?

JOHNNY FIVE

Yup.

MINUTES LATER

Llewyn is leaned back in the front passenger seat, its door open. His eyes are closed.

The sound of a distant door.

He looks out: Roland Turner is rounding the corner of the building, herky-jerking towards the car, slower than on his walk in.

Johnny Five unperches from the building and goes to help.

INT. CAR

Traveling. Minutes later.

Quiet. Llewyn looks back.

Roland Turner is in the back seat, eyes closed again. A trace of drool.

Johnny Five drives, smoking cigarette on his lip.

LLEWYN

So you're a friend of Al's?

JOHNNY FIVE

Yeah.

More driving.

INT. CAR − LATER

Point-of-view traveling forward. Guitar and singing at the cut-in.

Back seat: Roland Turner's jiggling, unconscious body.

Front seat: Llewyn plays and sings. He finishes the chorus, then looks to Johnny with a big nod of encouragement.

GREEN, GREEN ROCKY ROAD

When I go by Baltimore
Need no carpet on my floor
You come along and follow me
We'll go down to Galilee

Howlin' green, green rocky road
You promenadin' green
Tell me who you love
Tell me who you love

See that crow up in the sky
He don't walk, he just fly
He don't walk, he don't run
Keep on flappin' to the sun
Little Miss Jane, you run to the wall

Don't you stumble, don't you fall
Don't you sing, don't you shout
When I say, you come runnin' out

Hooka dooka, soda cracker
If your mama chew tobacker
If your mama chews tobacker
Hooka dooka, soda cracker

When I go by Baltimore
Need no carpet on my floor
You come along, follow me
There's a man in Galilee
He don't walk, he just fly
He don't walk, he don't run
Keep on flappin' to the sun

LLEWYN

All together now!

He reprises the chorus with gusto.

Johnny Five, unenlisted, drives on with no change of expression.

95

Llewyn is driving now. Johnny Five has his head back in the front passenger seat, asleep; in back, Roland Turner has woken up and then some.

> ROLAND TURNER

− a sign that said, "No massé shots no coins on cloth." I said "Am I allowed to bank the ball off the cushion or is that too fancy?" The guy says, "You're a hustler." I say, "You're a fucking idiot. A hustler pretends he's out of his depth, I'm telling you I'm an adept. Maybe you're the hustler just pretending to be a lunkhead. Got me fooled."

His cane head raps Llewyn's shoulder.

Hey Cowboy Chords! This would interest you. What do you think they make billiard balls out of now that the importation of ivory is illegal?

> LLEWYN

Couldn't tell you.

> ROLAND TURNER

Clay. But! Not just any fucking clay, Belgian clay. They have this clay – what did you say your name was?

> LLEWYN

Llewyn.

> ROLAND TURNER

That's right. They have this clay, only place in the world they can find it, just outside of Bruges. Harder than my dick if it's fired properly. Throw it against a wall. Many times as you want, go ahead, Elwyn, you ain't gonna break those little bastards. No massé shots, no coins on cloth. My ass. Girl Scout rules. Like music: you play like you play. Well you don't. But in jazz, you know, we play all the notes. Twelve notes in a scale, dipshit. Not three chords on a ukulele.

An assaultive drone:

Geeee . . . . Geeee . . . . Ceeee . . . . Geee . . . Ceeee . . . Deee . . . . Gee. Jesus fucking Christ. Well, if you make a living at it more power to you. Solo act?

LLEWYN

Yeah. Now.

ROLAND TURNER

Now? Used to, what, work with the cat? Every time you
played a C major it'd puke a hairball?

LLEWYN

I used to have a partner.

ROLAND TURNER

What happened?

LLEWYN

He threw himself off the George Washington Bridge.

Beat.

ROLAND TURNER

Well shit, I don't blame him, I couldn't take it either having
to play "Jimmie Crack Corn" every night. Although, pardon
me for saying so, but that's pretty fucking stupid isn't it?
George *Washington* Bridge? You throw yourself off the
Brooklyn Bridge. Traditionally. George *Washington* Bridge,
who does that? What was he, a dumbbell?

LLEWYN

Not really.

ROLAND TURNER

And that's when you picked up the cat? Thank God I never
had to resort to gimmicks. People pay to see Roland Turner.
Playing what he plays, going where he goes. Exploring. It's
the freedom they're paying to see. They don't wanna see
some jackass playing a song they've heard eighteen hundred
times before. Though if you make a living at it more power
to you.

The cane whacks Llewyn's shoulder again.

Here, this would interest you. There was this act I saw in
Montreux, Switzerland – bass, piano, and sound tree –

LLEWYN

Mr. Turner, I'm wondering.

ROLAND TURNER

Huh?

LLEWYN

Would that cane fit all the way up your ass or would a little stay sticking out?

Roland Turner stares at him.

ROLAND TURNER

Okay. Okay. Except threats and intimidation won't work with me and do you want to know why? This would interest you. I studied Santeria and certain other things that squares like you would call the black arts, due to lack of understanding, from Chano Pozzo in New Orleans. You say you'll mess me up? I don't have to make those childish threats, I just do my thing. I do my thing and one day you wake up wondering why do I have this pain in my side? I stretch and I eat right and I take warm baths but it just won't go away, this pain, why is that? Or maybe it won't even be that specific, depends, maybe it's just "Why is nothing going right for me?" Doesn't matter what I do, it just won't come out, I just can't make anything come out right. My life is a big bowl of shit. I don't *remember* making this big bowl of shit. And meantime, Roland Turner is somewhere a thousand miles away laughing his ass off. That's what happens.

A beat.

Think about *that*, Elwyn. In *this* car, bad manners won't work. Your turn to pay for the gas.

EXT. GAS STATION

Roland Turner is herky-jerking away into the background.

Johnny Five is once again in the driver's seat, Llewyn in the passenger seat. Llewyn's look shifts from the receding jazzman to Johnny Five.

LLEWYN

Bum a cigarette?

JOHNNY FIVE

I'm out.

Roland Turner recedes: clack-clack . . . clack-clack . . .

LATER

Tire chirp as the car pulls out of the station.

INT. CAR

Roland Turner asleep, drooling.

Llewyn, in the passenger seat, is looking at:

Johnny Five driving. A cigarette burns on his lower lip.

LLEWYN

You a musician?

A faint smile curls Johnny Five's lip. After a beat:

JOHNNY FIVE

I act.

LLEWYN

. . . In talkies?

LATER

Same driving configuration. Roland Turner still asleep.

We seem to have caught Johnny Five in a long beat between thoughts. He shrugs, pulls the cigarette from his lip and stubs it out.

He exhales smoke.

His eyes remain on the road as he speaks.

JOHNNY FIVE

Willowwall Carnival. Also.

A beat.

The Brig.

Another long beat staring at the road.

Three weeks on that show. Coulda been more. Cops closed it.

A beat while Llewyn waits for him to elaborate, but he doesn't. Llewyn prompts:

                    LLEWYN
How come?

                    JOHNNY FIVE
Nudity.

Long beat.

Cloves of Spring. Not a play. There was this French writer? Paul Verlaine? It was him.

Beat.

Him adapted. Then. Clean Asshole Poems. Orlovsky.

Driving beat.

Study too. Acting. Artaud. Grotowski. That stuff.

He shakes a cigarette out of a pack of Camels.

It's about trust.

He shrugs.

The moment.

ROAD

The car rips into frame and into the background.

CAR — LATER

Close on Roland Turner from outside his window as he gazes out, wearing sunglasses. His mouth hangs open as he watches the world go by, looking haunted.

Late day, gray day. One raindrop hits the window and is jitteringly dragged back by the wind.

Another raindrop.

Roland Turner's hand rises to pull off the sunglasses which he folds and slides into a pocket, still gazing out.

Another raindrop.

INT. OASIS DINER — FULL NIGHT

Thunderstorm outside. Muted inside. The foul weather, or the late hour, makes for not much clientele.

Roland Turner and Johnny Five and Llewyn sit at a booth set against plate glass. The Oasis sits on a highway overpass: through the rain-speckled window we see the blur of headlights and tail lights of traffic whirring by below.

The remains of a hot open-face roast beef sandwich sit before Roland Turner, who has his head pitched back, listening, as Johnny Five reads aloud from a book.

> JOHNNY FIVE
> "More more more, cried the bed – talk to me more –
> Oh bed that taked the weight of the world –
> All the lost dreams laid on you
> Oh bed that grows no hair, that cannot be fucked
> Or can be fucked
> Oh bed crumbs of all ages spilled on you
> Oh bed."

He draws on his cigarette, nodding, still looking at the book.

He closes the book.

He nods, looking at the closed book.

Still looking up at the ceiling:

> ROLAND TURNER
> Yesssss.

A beat.

> Well . . .

He stirs, looks about, grabs his canes.

Excuse me.

He hoists himself with a grunt and clacks away across the nearly deserted restaurant.

LLEWYN AT THE REGISTER

The cash register's ring-open hits the cut.

A waitress takes Llewyn's cash and makes change.

> LLEWYN
> How far are we from Chicago?

> WAITRESS
> Three hours. A little more, this weather.

TABLE

Johnny Five sits alone, elbow on table and hand up, extended thumb propped against his temple and burning cigarette wedged between two fingers. He stares with a quizzical expression at the book he once again reads. His mouth hangs open.

Llewyn is arriving back at the table. He drops some change on the tabletop.

> JOHNNY FIVE
> Ha ha ha ha ha!

With his eyes still on the book, Johnny Five's mirth mellows into a smile. The smile slowly fades. His mouth once again hangs open as he reads on.

Llewyn looks at the empty throw of restaurant.

MEN'S ROOM

Llewyn enters.

A clean, empty, fairly high-ceilinged bathroom with a long row of urinals and a long row of stalls.

Roland Turner's legs are visible beneath the door of one the nearer stalls.

Mindful of privacy, Llewyn goes a few stalls over and bumps its door open.

INSIDE THE STALL

Llewyn lowers himself into close shot.

He sits for a beat, waiting for things to develop.

His eyes idly shift. His look catches on something:

Grafitti on the partition wall:

> What are you doing!

Llewyn gazes at it.

There is the sound of slithering fabric ending with a flop-thump that echoes on the tile.

Llewyn frowns. He starts to rise.

BATHROOM

Llewyn emerges from his stall and goes to the other occupied stall. Roland Turner is partly visible lying on the floor. Part of an arm is visible: coat off, sleeve pushed up, hose wrapped.

He is face-up head toward us so that the top half of his face is visible. He is unconscious, eyes rolled up, sheened with sweat. He twitches.

MEN'S ROOM – LATER

Door.

Banging in at the cut.

Llewyn reenters the bathroom leading Johnny Five.

Roland Turner is twitching more violently.

LLEWYN
You stay with him, I'll call an ambulance.

Johnny Five, unconcerned, flicks the match with which he has lit a fresh cigarette.

JOHNNY FIVE

Nah, he's fine.

He goes for the body.

Grab his sticks.

DINER

Johnny Five has one of Roland Turner's arms draped over his shoulder and is helping him – all but hauling him – toward the door. Llewyn follows with his canes.

PARKING LOT

Johnny Five is easing Roland Turner into the back seat of the car.

The displaced cat walks circles around the part of the seat still unoccupied.

Llewyn dumps in the canes with a clatter.

The door is slammed shut.

RAMP EXITING OASIS

We are looking up at the glowing Oasis which sits on a highway overpass. Roland Turner's car descends toward us to merge back onto the highway. Its headlights show that it is still misting out.

DRIVING

Johnny Five gazes out, driving one-handed, cigarette on his lip.

His free hand fiddles the radio knob.

Very intermittent headlight-bys, accompanied by the whoosh of tires on wet asphalt.

Whining static hisses into music as Johnny finds a live station.

The thud of our car's wheels on road seams.

Llewyn eases his head back against the headrest.

Johnny Five starts humming along with a pop song.

Fade out picture and sound.

In black:

A silent beat broken by a sharp thwack-thwack: metal against glass.

Close on Llewyn opening his eyes.

The car is parked. It is still night.

Llewyn looks to his left:

Johnny Five is also stirring. Past him, a sweep of light ends with another thwack: a flashlight rapping against the driver's window.

Johnny rolls it down. Our view from the passenger's side crops the head of the leather-jacketed cop standing outside.

The wheels of a passing car whoosh by behind the cop: we are lower than the roadbed, pulled off on a shoulder.

The cop shines his light into Johnny Five's face.

> VOICE
>
> What're you doing?

Johnny Five recoils from the light.

> JOHNNY FIVE
>
> What? We're just –

> VOICE
>
> Can't stop here.

> JOHNNY FIVE
>
> I just pulled over to rest a minute.

> VOICE
>
> Are you inebriated?

> LLEWYN
>
> He's not drunk.

The cop briefly dips his head and shines the flashlight in at Llewyn.

COP

I didn't ask you. You, get out of the car.

JOHNNY FIVE

Me?

COP

You. Get out of the car.

Johnny Five opens the door, gets out.

C'mere.

The cop grabs him by the upper arm.

I want you to walk this –

*From Llewyn's point-of-view: Johnny Five shakes the hand off.
The two torsos are raked by a twirl of white light as the flashlight is*

dropped. A confusion of body parts as the officer regrabs Johnny and Johnny violently swings his arm away. Johnny's body is spun and slammed into the car chest-first.

Llewyn recoils at the impact.

Johnny's arms are being twisted behind his back. He is yanked away.

Llewyn's look follows, view half obscured by car body and sleeping Roland Turner in the back seat.

Johnny is frogmarched, hands cuffed behind his back, toward and past the headlights of a car parked behind. Its slowly turning gumball light sketchily shows the cop opening the back door, putting his hand on top of Johnny's head to sit him in, then climbing in front.

After a beat the siren fires up and the police car lurches into gear and bumps up onto the road, spitting shoulder gravel. It hangs a hard U-turn.

Red tail lights grow smaller. The siren recedes.

Llewyn's look shifts from back window to back seat.

Roland Turner sleeps on, breathing softly, sweating lightly.

The disturbed cat walks back and forth on the seat.

The whoosh of another car-by.

Llewyn's look wanders forward.

The ignition: no key.

Llewyn looks around, not for anything in particular. He shakes his head.

A still beat, thinking.

He decides.

He opens his door, gets out, closes the door.

He opens the back door, gets out his guitar and bag, hesitates.

The cat is seated now, looking up at him.

Beat.

Llewyn closes the door.

He mounts the shoulder to the road.

Sparse traffic both ways. Headlights hit him from front, from back. The backlight shows his breath vaporizing.

He takes a few steps in the direction the parked car was pointed, glances back.

His point-of-view: the car, a toppy view since it sits on a low shoulder. Dark inside.

Back to Llewyn. A few more steps. A car is approaching: he walks backwards, sticking out his thumb.

Black.

OUTLYING CHICAGO — DAWN

Fade in:

Wide: a car pulls over on a highway shoulder. Llewyn emerges, pulls his guitar and bag from the back seat.

Down from the shoulder a little ditch separates highway from broad weedy verge. Further still is a service road and on it a CTA bus terminus: fenced-in lot with a bus shelter outside of it.

Wind blows. The verge is patched with old snow.

The car pulls away and Llewyn goes down the shoulder, wades into the grass clogging the ditch, tries to hop and jump over the lowest point.

We hear a liquid squish.

LLEWYN
Goddamnit.

He comes grimacing up the other side.

Goddamn. Shit. Fuck.

He looks down at shoes and cuffs, soaked through.

Goddamn piss.

He crunches across crusted snow patches toward the bus stop.

BUS INTERIOR

Llewyn is one of two passengers in the parked bus.

Suddenly its public address sounds.

The driver, talking into his handset, says something about the route unintelligible through the PA.

The other passenger sits reading a newspaper, not listening.

The driver muscles the door shut and puts the bus in motion.

BUS — LATER

Through the window at Llewyn. The bus is now crowded. The window reflection shows downtown Chicago.

CHOCK FULL O' NUTS COUNTER

Walla and dish-clatter bang in at the cut.

We are on a side-on long-lens close-up of Llewyn. He has a cup of coffee. Stacked up beyond him are the morning-rush customers – all men, all in suits, some in overcoats. Foreground body parts of more men in suits.

Cut down to Llewyn's feet. He has slipped one shoe off and is now using his wet stockinged toes to pry off the other shoe so that his feet can dry.

Up to Llewyn drinking coffee.

Back down to his feet again. Both stockinged now, they relax onto the raised footrest whose black, ribbed-rubber surface is itself wet and filthy. The feet draw back, nudge the shoes into place so that they may rest upon them.

The waitress comes by.

                    WAITRESS
    More coffee?

                    LLEWYN
    Thanks.

CHOCK FULL O' NUTS PUBLIC PHONE

Phone book.

One of a pair of very thick books bound in pebbled black posterboard, sharing a pivot rod. The one is swung up to flop open in the middle.

Llewyn is at the public phone in the coffeeshop.

He flips pages.

We see him find the listing. In bold face that distinguishes it from the listings for private residences: GATE OF HORN.

Llewyn dials.

It rings through.

As Llewyn listens to it ring he copies the street address onto the front of his newspaper.

Several rings.

He hangs up.

CHOCK FULL O' NUTS COUNTER

Llewyn sits back in. The counter is now nearly empty.

> WAITRESS
>
> We're switching over.

> LLEWYN
>
> Huh?

> WAITRESS
>
> We're switching over to lunch service. And my shift is up.
> Can you pay the ticket?

CHICAGO STREET

Llewyn walks, guitar over his back, one hand carrying bag, the other clutching his corduroy jacket closed at his neck. It is blowing hard.

TRAIN STATION

Echoing interior.

A big institutional clock: 12:15.

Llewyn sits into frame side-on, onto a tall-backed wooden bench, eyes up at the clock.

He leans his head back against the wooden back, closes his eyes.

After a beat a Commuter sits into frame in the foreground.

> COMMUTER
> You hear that about the South Bend train?

Llewyn opens his eyes.

> LLEWYN
> What?

> COMMUTER
> You hear that announcement? How long is it delayed?

> LLEWYN
> No. Don't know.

The man rises and leaves.

Llewyn closes his eyes again.

Soft, in the background, a man in a blue uniform is looking at Llewyn. A moment of hesitation, then he walks toward us and Llewyn, growing sharper but head cropping out the top of frame.

> COP'S VOICE
> What train you waiting for?

Llewyn's eyes open again. He looks for a wordless beat.

Another prompt:

COP'S VOICE

Got a ticket?

A beat of Llewyn's sullen stare.

EXT. GATE OF HORN

Its exterior sign. Below the name of the club:

> *Folk Music*
> *Jazz*
> *Charcoal Sandwiches*

It is late afternoon. Llewyn goes to the front door and tries it. It is locked.

He rattles it, then drops his bag and cups his hands at the window to try to see in.

He steps back, looks to either side.

BACK OF CLUB

There is a stage door. Llewyn pushes on it: it gives.

INT. CLUB

The house is dark. Llewyn has entered from just off a little stage.

LLEWYN

Hello?

There is an office door ajar in back. A young man sticks his head out.

MAN

Hello?

LLEWYN

Is Bud Grossman here?

MAN

Isn't in yet.

The person disappears back into the office.

Llewyn looks around, a little lost. He projects:

LLEWYN

Can I wait here?

From inside the office:

VOICE

Sure. Maybe an hour.

LATER

Llewyn has one of the chairs down off a table and his guitar out and is playing, idling.

The scrape of the stage door. Llewyn stops playing.

Bud Grossman enters, stamping off snow. He has a nice coat.

He walks toward the back, past Llewyn, noticing him but not interested.

Llewyn, perhaps waiting for Bud Grossman to speak first, now watches him pass and disappear into the back office.

Murmur of voices.

Llewyn leans the guitar against the table, picks up his bag and goes back to the office door.

BACK OFFICE

Bud Grossman and the young man we saw earlier look up from their conversation.

LLEWYN

Mr. Grossman?

A beat.

BUD GROSSMAN

Yeah?

LLEWYN

I, uh. I'm Llewyn Davis.

A beat.

BUD GROSSMAN

Uh-huh.

LLEWYN

I'm sorry – do you know me?

BUD GROSSMAN

No.

LLEWYN

Mel Novikoff sent you my record, maybe a month ago,
"Inside Llewyn Davis" –

BUD GROSSMAN

Oh, you're with Mel?

LLEWYN

Yeah, I was in Chicago – just passing through, uh – Do you
like the record?

BUD GROSSMAN

Don't know. Didn't get it.

Llewyn digs in his bag.

LLEWYN

Here it is, this is it anyway. It's, here it is.

Bud Grossman takes it, looks at it.

That's five dollars.

Bud Grossman doesn't react.

He looks up from the record. Llewyn holds his look for a beat.

. . . I was joking.

BUD GROSSMAN

Uh-huh.

A beat.

LLEWYN

Well, I'm interested in maybe gigging here but also in obtaining management –

BUD GROSSMAN

Getting any money out of Mel?

LLEWYN

Not, uh . . . not, uh –

BUD GROSSMAN

Yeah, I'll bet.

The faintest smile fades. He shrugs.

Okay. Let's hear something.

LLEWYN

. . . You don't want to listen to the record?

BUD GROSSMAN

Why should I, you're here. Play me something.

He looks down at the record.

Play me something from . . . "Inside Llewyn Davis."

LLEWYN

Okay. Here? Stage?

BUD GROSSMAN

Not here.

ONSTAGE – A MINUTE LATER

Onstage, guitar in one hand, Llewyn swings a chair into place with the other.

He sits, puts the guitar on his knee.

Bud Grossman sits near the front of the mostly-dark house.

Llewyn looks at him, looks at the guitar. A beat.

LLEWYN

Okay.

He plays.

THE DEATH OF QUEEN JANE

Queen Jane lay in labor full nine days or more
Till her women grew so tired, they could no longer there
They could no longer there

"Good women, good women, good women as you be
Will you open my right side and find my baby
And find my baby"

"Oh no," cried the women, "that's a thing that can never be
We will call on King Henry and hear what he may say
And hear what he may say"

King Henry was sent for, King Henry did come
Saying, "What does ail you, my lady? Your eyes, they look
 so dim
Your eyes, they look so dim"

"King Henry, King Henry, will you do one thing for me?
Will you open my right side and find my baby
And find my baby"

"Oh no," cried King Henry, "that's a thing that I can never do
If I lose the Flower of England, I shall lose the branch too
I shall lose the branch too"

There was fiddling and dancing on the day the babe was born
But poor Queen Jane beloved, she lay cold as a stone
Lay cold as a stone

He finishes the song.

He looks out at Bud Grossman.

Bud Grossman has yet to show any reaction, to anything.

A good beat, and then:

BUD GROSSMAN
I don't see a lot of money here.

At length:

                              LLEWYN
     Okay.

Another beat. Bud Grossman doesn't get up, neither does Llewyn.

     Okay. That's it?

Bud Grossman shrugs a "What else would there be?"

                          BUD GROSSMAN
     You're okay. You're not green.

Llewyn nods at the compliment, such as it is. He hesitates; then:

                              LLEWYN
     But I don't have what, say, Troy Nelson has.

For the first time, Bud Grossman seems pleasantly interested:

                          BUD GROSSMAN
     You know Troy?

                              LLEWYN
     Yeah.

                          BUD GROSSMAN
     Good kid. (*Nods thoughtfully.*) Good kid.

Llewyn rises. Bud Grossman continues:

     . . . Yeah, he connects with people.

Bud Grossman watches Llewyn stowing his guitar.

     Look, I'm putting together a trio. Two guys and a girl
     singer. You're no front guy but if you can grow a goatee,
     stay out of the sun, we might see how your voice works
     with the other two. Comfortable with harmonies?

                              LLEWYN
     No. Yes, but, no. I had a partner.

                          BUD GROSSMAN
     Uh-huh, well that makes sense. My suggestion? Get back
     together.

That's good advice. Thank you, Mr. Grossman.

SNOW-PATCHED MEDIAN — LATE DAY

The bus terminal is in the background. A very low, very weak, grayed-out sun hangs at the horizon. The wind blows hard.

Llewyn is negotiating the ditch, coming toward the foreground highway, guitar across his back and bag in hand.

SAME — SEVERAL MINUTES LATER

Now dusk: some ambient light but the cars all have headlights on. It has started to snow.

A car pulls over to where Llewyn stands with his thumb out. A crew-cut college-age Youth leans over to roll down the passenger window and look up at him.

YOUTH

Where you going?

LLEWYN

New York.

YOUTH

Man, that's great! I'm going home to New Jersey, I have not slept – you drive, right?

LLEWYN

Yeah.

YOUTH

Well as long as you drive and let me sleep, we can do it all the way, man! Put your cello in back.

Llewyn opens the back door to stow his gear. The Youth unstraps his seat belt and slides over to the passenger side.

You're not gonna try to talk to me?

LLEWYN

No. Just show me the knob for the windshield wipers.

FULL NIGHT

A point-of-view: heavier snow swirls into headlights and sticks soft and dark to the foreground windshield. The wipers, beating a soporific thid-thud, take it away.

Passenger seat: the crew-cut Youth, asleep. Regular, heavy breathing.

Llewyn driving. Bedraggled.

Llewyn looks around the dash, locates, and reaches.

The radio goes on. The tuner is thumbed through static hiss. Coming through it, finally, distant music. Knob-fiddling cannot make clear. More exploring. Radio off.

Llewyn blinks himself more awake. He reacts to something he sees:

Hinging point-of-view of approaching sign: it marks the turnoff for Akron.

Llewyn's head turns as he tracks the sign. His eyes shift in the direction of the sign's arrow.

A glow through the snow of distant city lights.

Back to Llewyn. His eyes hold on the ghost of the city for a brief beat, then shift forward.

He drives.

Fade out.

LATER

Still snowing.

As he drives Llewyn sings, half aloud, "Ladies of Spain."

A glance over at:

The Youth, still sleeping deeply.

A look forward – and a startled reaction:

Almost as soon as we see it, movement in the headlights is lost below the hood.

Impact thud. Squeal of brakes.

Llewyn rocks forward at the hard brake and so does the Youth, who then flops back. His deep breathing continues undisturbed.

Llewyn takes a wide-eyed moment. He looks around through the back window.

Nothing is visible outside except dimly falling snow.

Llewyn opens his door.

EXT. SNOWY ROAD – NIGHT

Driver's side headlight in the foreground. Blood on the bumper.

Llewyn is walking into the foreground to look. A looking beat. He recedes into the background.

He stands behind the idling car, looking at the highway behind.

No traffic, peaceful, dark, falling snow. Nothing visible on the road.

Llewyn's look travels.

Something catches his eye.

Movement, perhaps thirty yards back, off the shoulder: a small animal?

Llewyn squints against snow.

A badger- or ferret-sized creature is hauling itself haltingly toward the woods that line the highway. Before we get a good look at it, it disappears into the dark of the trees.

CAR INTERIOR

Llewyn sits in.

The engine rumbles in park.

The wipers thud.

The Youth breathes in and out.

After a beat, Llewyn puts the car in gear.

ROAD

Locked-down: the car pulls away from us, into the background. Tail lights recede, leave us in falling snow.

SUBWAY CAR

Loud train clatter bangs in at the cut.

No time of day: we are underground. Llewyn sits in a mostly empty car, still with guitar and bag, still – judging by his haggardness, the most extreme yet – sleepless.

EARLY MORNING

Close on Llewyn asleep.

Early morning – somewhere.

Llewyn emerges from peaceful sleep. He rolls onto his back, looking up.

Cottage-cheese ceiling, underlit by light leaking around a curtain.

Llewyn rises to an elbow, looks around, orienting himself.

A child's room. He is in a child's bed.

A plastic red-framed something on the nightstand at his elbow: he picks it up.

An Etch-a-Sketch. Written on it in the spidery way permitted by the device:

> *Welcome Uncle Llewyn*

EXT. JOY'S HOUSE — MORNING

Llewyn emerges from his sister's Queens house.

INT. GREAT HALL

Cut in with a crash of echoing walla. It is the interior hall of a once-grand beaux-art institution gone to seed.

Llewyn sits at the battered wooden desk of an aging man who seems more working-class than bureaucrat.

                              MAN
        No you cannot.

                            LLEWYN
        Why?

                              MAN
        Ya not on the rosta.

                            LLEWYN
        Well, okay. Can you put me on the roster?

                              MAN
        Me? No I cannot.

                            LLEWYN
        Why?

                              MAN
        Why ya think?

LLEWYN

I don't know. Because I'm a communist.

The man, suddenly less bored, glances around and then leans in, voice lowered:

MAN

Shachmanite?

LLEWYN

What?

MAN
(*"my mistake"*)

Nah, no. It ain't that. Y'ain't current.

LLEWYN

I'm not *current*.

MAN

That's another way of puttin it.

LLEWYN

Is that a nautical term?

MAN

Y'ain't *current*, on ya dues. Pay ya dues, ya go back on the rosta, I can ship ya out. There's a post on *The Maid of the Gate*, Seaman First Class, weighs anchor this Friday 6 p.m.

Llewyn is looking in his wallet.

LLEWYN

The money, what I owe, can't they take it out of, whatever, the first week? I can't run out on it, I'm in your fucking sardine can.

MAN

Yeah, they don't do that. Ya gotta be current to ship out.

Llewyn finishes thumbing through his wallet.

LLEWYN

Okay. Wow. I just make it. I'm leaving naked, man. Clean start. Can I pay you?

MAN

Yeah. I'll write ya a receipt. And the pier and ship number,
and the time. Still got ya Masters Mates and Pilots License,
right? Ain't shippin out without that.

LLEWYN

Yeah, I got it.

MAN

Okay. Here it is. "Llewyn Davis." Ya not Hugh's kid are ya?

LLEWYN

Why not.

EXT. RETIREMENT HOUSE

Ocean.

*Looking out at gray ocean and gray sky. Waves beat weakly against
foreground rocky shore.*

*A building: a hulking brick institutional building facing the water.
Over a rectilinear portico is the building's name: Landfall.*

INSIDE

*A card set into a metal frame on a tile wall, next to an interior door.
Below the card is a glass display box. On the card, in marker:*

Hugh Davis

*Inside the box are little personal mementos and snapshots. Some of the
photos show an old man in a sweater with a grandson, and with
grandson and Joy and a man presumably Joy's husband. There is also
a ship-in-the-bottle inside the display box, and a few greeting cards.*

From off, the sound of a door being pushed open.

INSIDE ROOM

As Llewyn enters with guitar case.

LLEWYN

Hiya.

132

Hugh Davis sits by the window, not looking out. He does look up at Llewyn's entrance.

Llewyn sets down his guitar and swings a chair around to face his father.

. . . How's it going.

No answer, but none, it seems, is expected.

. . . Taking off, Pop. Won't see you for a while, shipping out.

His father's look rests upon him, but not with much expression.

A beat of looking at each other.

Llewyn rises, not uncomfortable, to look out the rib-height window.

. . . Try something new.

He looks out for a beat.

. . . I mean, something old.

His point-of-view: parking lot, some marshy grass, ocean. He shrugs, looking out. He sits back down.

. . . How's it going.

The old man's eyes have followed him back and forth.

Llewyn leans forward to unclasp the guitar case. He withdraws the guitar.

LLEWYN
. . . Okay, here's this. You used to like this.

He limbers his fingers briefly, then plays, and sings "The Shoals of Herring."

THE SHOALS OF HERRING

O, it was a fine and a pleasant day
Out of Yarmouth Harbor I was faring
As a cabin boy on a sailing lugger
For to hunt the bonny shoals of herring

Well, I earned my keep and I paid my way
And I earned the gear that I was wearing

133

Sailed a million miles, caught ten million fishes
That we'd hunted in the shoals of herring

Night and day, the seas were daring
Come, wind, O call our winter gale
Sweating or cold, growing up
Growing old or dying
As we hunt the bonny shoals of herring

The old man watches him sing. Once, even, his eyes shift to look at the guitar fingering.

The old man's eyes shift, dreamily, to the window. They hold there for a long beat, then return to Llewyn as the song finishes. The last chord is held, and rings out. The two men look at each other, lost, it seems, in the music as it floats away.

A long beat, and then, from Llewyn:

> LLEWYN
> *(softly)*

. . . Wow.

Another silent beat, and a more definite:

. . . Wow.

He realizes he still holds the guitar and stirs, leans forward to lay it gently in its case, and rises.

HALLWAY

Wide, looking the length of the hall with sun glaring on the linoleum and streaking the tile walls. Llewyn emerges from his father's room small, in the background, without the guitar.

Emerged fully into the hall he stops, and looks briefly up and down its length.

He walks toward us, head turning to look into the rooms he passes.

We jump in on his walk as he checks to the side, and then stops:

A young black orderly is making a bed in an empty room.

LLEWYN

Excuse me.

The man looks up.

. . . Can I . . . trouble you . . . My father, uh, had an accident and uh . . . might need some help . . . He needs to be cleaned.

QUEENS HOUSE

Llewyn enters with his guitar. His sister is in the kitchen at the stove, and a six-year-old sits eating at the table.

JOY

How is he?

LLEWYN

He's great. Good to see what I have to look forward to.

JOY

What? Llewyn.

LLEWYN

No, I'm not kiddin. I've got it all figured out now. Put in some hard years, yeah, but eventually ya get to kick back, your food brought to ya, don't even have to get up to shit.

JOY

Llewyn! Danny is sitting right here!

LLEWYN

I'm sorry.

JOY

What is wrong with you! Shame on you!

LLEWYN

I'm sorry. It was good to see him. It was great. Where'd you put my file box?

JOY

Huh?

LLEWYN

From the house, where's my file box?

She stares at him.

JOY

You told me to throw everything out.

He stares back.

LLEWYN

All the *old* stuff! Fuck, Joy, you threw out my file box?

JOY

Llewyn!

LLEWYN

Yeah, no cursing, except now I gotta go back to the fucking union hall! It had my Masters Mates and Pilots license, Jesus *Christ*, Joy!

She comes close so that Danny won't hear. A fierce whisper:

> JOY
> You told me to put it out by the curb. It's what I did. I want you to leave. Get outta heah.

Angry, not apologetic:

> LLEWYN
> Fuck. Yeah. I know, I'm a *dick*, right?

> JOY
> That's right.

Llewyn looks at the eating child.

> LLEWYN
> Danny, your uncle's a bad man.

> DANNY
> Okay.

BERKEY'S FOYER DIRECTORY

The familiar glass-covered tenant listing, showing BERKEY 6C.

A finger enters to buzz.

Filtered:

> JEAN
> Hello?

Wider on the foyer as Llewyn, guitar on back and bag in hand, leans in to a round mesh grille:

> LLEWYN
> It's Llewyn, don't hang up I don't wanna stay, I just need a place to dump my stuff please, I'm tired of dragging it all around with me.

HALLWAY

Llewyn goes to the apartment door.

BERKEY APARTMENT

As Jean lets Llewyn into the apartment. She indicates where the bags may be stowed:

JEAN

Under the couch. Where you gonna stay?

LLEWYN

I don't know, I only need two nights, there must be someone in the five boroughs who isn't pissed at me. How do you feel?

JEAN

Fine. Why?

LLEWYN

I'm sorry. So it went okay?

JEAN

I'm doing it *Saturday*. Jesus, Llewyn, you don't even fucking remember?

LLEWYN

Oh, yeah, boy. I've been away – seemed like a long time but I guess it was only a couple days, yeah. Yeah. Sorry.

JEAN

Where were you?

LLEWYN

Chicago.

JEAN

Why?

He shakes his head, gropes.

LLEWYN

Nah, nothin.

JEAN

Pappi'll let you play tomorrow, pick up a couple bucks.

LLEWYN

No he won't, I was there less than a month ago.

JEAN

He will. I asked him.

LLEWYN

Well. Thank you. That was nice of you. But I'm out, I'm done. Going back to the merchant marine.

JEAN

What? That's it? (*He shrugs.*) This could be good for you, tomorrow.

LLEWYN

Playing the Gaslight for the four-hundredth time? Really? For the fucking basket?

JEAN

Um. You'd have to split the basket, there's another act.

Llewyn laughs.

But the *Times* is gonna be there.

LLEWYN

Big fuckin deal! I'm sorry – Thanks for the thought. It's not going anywhere, and I'm tired.

JEAN

You're tired.

LLEWYN

I am so fucking tired. I thought I just needed a night's sleep but it's more than that. But thank you. For trying. I love you.

This gets a genuine laugh from Jean.

JEAN

Oh, come on.

UNION HALL – DAY

Low shot.

Llewyn in the union hall.

LLEWYN

Are you shitting me?

A different old geezer than in the first visit.

MAN

In what way, buddy?

LLEWYN

Eighty-five dollars. To replace the license.

MAN

You don't t'row out the license. That's the one thing you keep.

LLEWYN

I can't – where'm I gonna . . . Fuhhh . . . Well . . . lemme get this money back then . . .

He is digging in his pocket.

I kept this fucking thing. I just paid my dues this morning, a hundred and forty-eight bucks, here's the receipt.

MAN

Huh? You don't . . . we don't pay you dues back. Wuddya nuts?

LLEWYN

I just paid it this morning! Four hours ago!

MAN

Yeah?

LLEWYN

Wait wait wait wait – you're saying I can't crew the ship, and I can't get this money back?

The geezer shrugs, looking at the receipt.

MAN

This was money you owed your union . . . Say, you Hugh Davis's kid?

LLEWYN

Yeah.

MAN

How's he doin?

LLEWYN

He's fucking great! Matter of fact he's been asking after you!

THE GASLIGHT — NIGHT

Four Irishmen in Aran Island sweaters are performing.

THE AULD TRIANGLE

A hungry feeling came o'er me stealing
And the mice were squealing in my prison cell
And the auld triangle went jingle-jangle
All along the banks of the Royal Canal

To begin the morning a screw was bawling
"Get up, you bowsie, and clean up your cell!"
And the auld triangle went jingle-jangle
All along the banks of the Royal Canal

The lags were sleeping, Humpy Gussy was creeping
As I lay there weeping for my girl Sal
And the auld triangle went jingle-jangle
All along the banks of the Royal Canal

Up in the female prison there's seventy-five women
And among them I wish I did dwell
Then the auld triangle could go jingle-jangle
All along the banks of the Royal Canal

*The house is full and some people watch leaning back against the bar.
Llewyn is the only person seated at the bar and facing it, glowering, a
drink in his fist.*

Pappi Corsicatto sits in, squeezing Llewyn's shoulder.

PAPPI

Hey. We gonna hear you tomorrow.

LLEWYN
(*no warmth*)

I guess you are.

141

PAPPI

Well – ya welcome.

No answer.

Wuddya think a these guys?

Llewyn swivels, drink still in hand, and looks darkly at the stage.

At length:

LLEWYN

I like the sweaters.

Pappi stares at the stage also, mouth open, nodding.

At length:

PAPPI

Ya know, you wouldn't fuckin believe the rent here. This folk shit, I don't know.

Both men stare at the stage.

. . . You know any comics?

A beat.

LLEWYN

Only you, Pappi.

PAPPI
(*modest*)

Aw, I couldn't puhfawm.

After a beat gazing at the stage, he waxes philosophical.

Comics, they don't look like much, most of 'em. Jews, by'n large. Lookin like that I guess ya gotta be funny. Some a' the folk acts on the otha hand, ya gotta give'm they look good. They look good at least. Jim and Jean we get a good crowd. You know why, Llewyn? A lotta these guys, a lot of 'em come in here catch the act because – they wanna fuck Jean. Is why they come in. And some of 'em. Some of these guys, Llewyn, they come in here cause they wanna fuck JIM! Heh heh heh! They wanna fuck Jim, know what I mean?

144

LLEWYN
You mean they wanna fuck Jim.

PAPPI
Exactly!

He nods.

Exactly. Well. (*Sighs.*) Me . . . I've only fucked Jean.

The Irish trio's song, and set, is ending, to applause. Pappi's line has brought Llewyn's look around from the stage.

LLEWYN
Huh?

Pappi is thumping his hands together for the trio.

PAPPI
Oh yeah. Oh yeah. Ya know. Ya wanna play the Gaslight . . .

Pappi shrugs.

Llewyn's look darkens further, and swings back to the stage.

IRISH SINGER
Thank you, ladies and gentlemen. Thank you . . . Thank you, Pappi Corsicatto, and let's all give a great big welcome to Elizabeth Hobby, from Elinora, Arkansas!

An older woman smiles thanks as she takes the stage with an autoharp. She has stringy blond hair and a gaunt face and frame, and her smile, though warm, shows that she is missing a tooth or two.

ELIZABETH HOBBY
Thank you, ladies and gentlemen. Yer so nice. Thank you. This is my first show in New York –

Llewyn bellows:

LLEWYN
How'd ya get the gig, Betty?

A few uncomprehending titters from the house.

Elizabeth Hobby, flustered, shades her eyes.

. . . Hello?

Llewyn, with a significant look to Pappi, points a finger at the woman onstage and cocks his head to pose a question.

Pappi Corsicatto laughs.

PAPPI
Aw c'mon, Llewyn, gimme a little credit.

ELIZABETH HOBBY
I'm gonna do a song, it's like most of the songs I do, it's a song I grew up with.

She starts playing and singing.

LLEWYN
Where's your haybale!

Looks and shushes from other customers.

. . . Where's your corncob pipe! Ya wearing gingham panties? Show us your panties!

PAPPI
C'mon, Llewyn. It's enough.

He shakes off Pappi's hand.

LLEWYN
I hate fucking *folk* music.

Pappi motions to the bartender.

PAPPI
Okay, Eddie. We might need Florio.

LLEWYN
Fuck Florio! Fuck *you*, Pappi!

FRONT OF THE GASLIGHT

Wide on the front of the club as Llewyn stumbles out, under impetus from the bartender and another man.

There is the beginnings of a line for the second set. Llewyn glares at the onlookers, and, as he starts to wander off:

LLEWYN
The show is bullshit. Four micks and Grandma Moses.

STREET

A phone booth seen in wide shot.

Wind blows, traffic goes by.

Llewyn is a small figure in the booth, not on the phone but looking down motionless, studying something held in one hand.

We jump in as he reaches for it with his other hand: his open address book. The hand turns the page, lingers for a moment, turns again.

GORFEINS' ELEVATOR

The elevator operator holds down the throttle. He looks back to Llewyn.

GORFEINS' HALLWAY / APARTMENT

Apartment door swings open.

Mitch Gorfein beams out.

MITCH
Llewyn, come on in! Lillian is making her famous tabouleh salad!

LLEWYN
Thanks, Mitch. I really appreciate this, after last time. I just can't tell you how sorry I –

MITCH
Oh forget it! We all get a little emotional over Mike. It comes out in different ways. He had such *life*. Such a talent. It's a big hole. A big hole.

LLEWYN
Yeah. Uh-huh.

MITCH

How long'll you be with us?

LLEWYN

Just a day or two, if it's okay. Just until I figure out the next, um . . . the next –

MITCH

This is Arlen and Dodi Gamble. This is Llewyn Davis, our folksinger friend. Arlen knows Jim Berkey.

ARLEN

You're Jim and Jean's friend!

LLEWYN

Well – sort of –

DODI

Jim played us a pressing of that record – "Please, Mr. Kennedy." It was hysterical.

ARLEN

So funny! That's gonna be a hit, man. Royalties on that, it's gonna pay out for a long time.

Llewyn stares, then nods, blankly.

LLEWYN

Uh-huh.

DODI

I wish I was in your business – one hit can fix you up!

LLEWYN

Uh. Yeah, I –

LILLIAN

Llewyn!

She enters, beaming, bearing a large bowl that she hastily places on the table so as to be able to hug Llewyn.

LLEWYN

Hi Lillian.

LILLIAN

I'm so sorry I upset you –

LLEWYN

No no! What, you're apologizing to me? Jesus, Lillian, I –
holy shit!

He breaks the embrace, looking off.

A cat has trotted in.

. . . Well – that's good. You got a new cat.

MITCH

No.

LILLIAN

He came home.

She scoops the cat up.

MITCH

He found his way back.

LILLIAN

The doorman heard something scratching yesterday morning.

MITCH

Early morning. Wee hours.

LILLIAN

See?

She is holding the cat up, belly out, by its forepaws.

. . . It's Ulysses.

Llewyn looks from the cat's scrotum to Lillian.

LLEWYN

It's what?

LILLIAN

Ulysses.

LLEWYN

I didn't, uh . . . That's its name?

GORFEINS' STUDY — LATER

Llewyn plops down onto the study couch. Lights are off. The apartment is quiet.

He digs into pockets to empty them onto the nightstand. Coins and tokens from one pocket. His wallet from another. He pokes through the bill compartment: six dollars.

He shakes his head, dumps it on the nightstand.

LATER STILL

Close on Llewyn, eyes closed, on his back, the regular breathing of deep sleep.

After a long beat: a soft thud and a "Huh!" of surprise from Llewyn as his body tenses and his eyes fly open.

After a moment to register where he is, he looks down his body.

Close on the cat, standing on his chest, looking back at him, purring loudly.

GORFEINS' APARTMENT — NEXT MORNING

Looking down the dim hall toward the less dim study.

Llewyn's head peeks out.

LLEWYN

Hello?

No answer.

He emerges to walk down the hallway in his undies.

COMMON HALLWAY

Outside the apartment door.

Llewyn emerges, dressed, and takes care with one foot to keep the cat hemmed in the apartment as he exits.

STREET — DAY

Llewyn is walking. After a beat his attention is caught by something to one side. He slows, looking, and stops.

His point-of-view. An illustration of a house cat. On either side of it is a dog. The three pets are out in the wild.

Llewyn looking.

Wider point-of-view: the illustration is a poster in a movie-theater lightbox, the theater not yet open.

It is a poster for The Incredible Journey. *The tag line promises "A Fantastic True-Life Drama."*

As Llewyn stares, music fades in: Llewyn himself, performing "Hang Me, Oh Hang Me."

CLUB – NIGHT

The music is a pre-lap of Llewyn in the Gaslight, spotlit as at the beginning of the movie.

HANG ME, OH HANG ME

Hang me, oh hang me, I'll be dead and gone
Hang me, oh hang me, I'll be dead and gone
I wouldn't mind the hanging, it's just the laying in the
    grave so long
Poor boy, I've been all around this world

He finishes the song to applause.

LLEWYN

Thank you. You've probably heard that one before, but what the hell. If it was never new, and it never gets old, then it's a folk song. One more before I go.

He performs "Fare Thee Well (Dink's Song)."

If I had wings like Nora's dove
I'd fly the river to the one I love
Fare thee well, O honey
Fare thee well

AT THE BAR

Pappi Corsicatto nods Llewyn over. He is broadly smiling.

PAPPI

Boy, you were some mess last night.

LLEWYN

Yeah, sorry, Pappi. I'm an asshole.

PAPPI

Oh, I don't give a shit. It's just music. Your friend is out back.

LLEWYN

My friend?

PAPPI

Guy in a suit?

A clatter offscreen attracts Llewyn's attention:

Backlit in the smoky spotlight a young man with a dutch-boy cap and a guitar and a harmonica on a rack is just sitting down onstage.

He blows a couple times on the harmonica.

BACK ALLEY

The steel door of the club swings open and Llewyn emerges. The man waiting against the wall:

> MAN
>
> You a funny boy, huh?

> LLEWYN
>
> What?

The man tosses his cigarette away and pushes himself off the wall.

> MAN
>
> Had to open ya big mouth, funny boy?

> LLEWYN
>
> Had to – what? It's what I do. For a living. Who're –

> MAN
>
> What ya do? Make fun a folks up there. Folks up there sangin?

> LLEWYN
>
> I'm sorry, *what?* I'm – oof!

The man has just socked him in the mouth.

> MAN
>
> You sit there in the audience last night yellin yer crap?

Llewyn is holding his mouth.

> LLEWYN
>
> Oh for Christ's sake. You yell stuff, it's a show.

> MAN
>
> Wasn't your show!

He hits him again and Llewyn goes down in the slush of the alleyway.

LLEWYN

It's not the opera, jackass!

He kicks. Llewyn curls into a defensive ball and bellows from behind protective forearms:

It's a fucking baskethouse!

The man kicks again.

MAN

We leavin this fuckin cesspool. You kin have it, smartass.

More kicking.

Yellin yer crap when my wife is up there tryin to sang! I took her home cryin!

The man strides off down the alley.

Llewyn stays balled up for a long moment. Once he is certain no more kicks are coming, he begins, slowly and painfully, to straighten out, exploring tender places with one hand.

The man has disappeared around the alley corner.

Llewyn rises experimentally to a crouch, straightens a little more. He takes a few uneven steps toward the mouth of the alley, one hand brushing the wall for balance.

Near the mouth of the alley he sinks back down to seated position, back against the wall, looking down the street in the direction the man exited.

The man is halfway down the block. He raises his hand and whistles down an oncoming cab. He climbs in.

After a short beat, the cab starts moving again.

As it passes the mouth of the alley, Llewyn touches two fingers to his forehead in salute.

LLEWYN

Au revoir.

The cab is past.

Its tail lights recede.

Cut to black.

A CONVERSATION WITH T BONE BURNETT

T Bone Burnett, the renowned musician who played on Bob Dylan's Rolling Thunder tour, is a songwriter and soundtrack and record producer, working with artists as varied as Roy Orbison, John Mellencamp, Elvis Costello and Diana Krall, Elton John, Tony Bennett, and many others. Burnett won Grammy Awards for the soundtrack of the Coen Brothers' film O Brother, Where Art Thou? *and for his work with Alison Krauss and Robert Plant. His song 'The Scarlet Tide' from* Cold Mountain *earned an Academy Award nomination. In 2010, Burnett won the Oscar for his song 'The Weary Kind' for the film* Crazy Heart. *He is currently producing the music for the ABC-TV show* Nashville. *In talking about his work as executive music producer on* Inside Llewyn Davis, *Burnett begins by discussing the film's significance:*

You know, it's a really important film to me, so . . .

Why do you feel that? Why is it important for you?

The film is about a time very much like the time we're in.

Can you explain that?

Well, I don't want to give a lot away. But you know, the film is about a time when there's a new moment happening. The old has died, and the new thing hasn't quite been born. We've been in an interregnum now for the past ten years, really, where the old has been dying but is not dead, and the new is being born but it's not yet alive.

We've been in this brackish water where it's not one thing or another. The old structure that we lived in for, you know, my whole lifetime has been dismantled for the most part. But the new, the new structure hasn't taken place. You realize this is an incredibly long conversation that has to do with, you know, everything that's going on in the internet, and in music.

I understand.

But at any rate, I feel we're at a time now when the value of music has been brought into question. And this movie speaks very eloquently, I think, about the value of music, and about the value of art throughout culture. We've been in a period of time, for the last twenty years really, during which there's been an assault on the arts by the technology community. The technology community has devalued the art, especially music, and has taken over the role of the artist in the society. We're being told now that artists are to crowd source their work, that artists are to follow the crowd rather than lead the crowd. Well, there's no artist worth his salt that will follow the crowd.

Of course.

I'm not interested in any artist who will follow the crowd. Jules Verne put a man on the moon a hundred years before a rocket scientist did. Einstein said that Picasso preceded him by twenty years. The arts have always led the sciences, and they should, too, because the arts are involved with the whole of humanity, the whole of the creation, not just specific parts of it. We can't let the engineers be in control of our society because one thing will happen. We will turn into the matrix. So that's why this film is important to me because it talks about this in a very eloquent way. So many arguments have been posed, so many cheap arguments have been floated out there, and they're still floating around our culture like, like a virus, exactly like a virus. As in "Information wants to be free." This film is a much more profound way to talk about where we are.

How do you see that issue in the movie in terms of the character Llewyn Davis and his story?

Well, you know, the thing is he's very good, but the thing he's doing – there's no line, there's no structure that supports what he's doing at all. He's completely out on his own. And that's where all musicians are today. Every musician in the world, you know. The irony of the internet, which was supposed to democratize everything, is that it's consolidated power even more so in the big media companies.

It's true.

And the individual artist that it was supposed to empower is essentially just putting a message in a bottle. There's no support system for anybody; so an artist – Llewyn in the film – can go to the record company and look for his royalties, but you know, there are no royalties because – they made one box of records and it's in the closet. That's the access the internet gives us.

That is exactly what happens to Llewyn. He's a serious musician and artist, and he has integrity but he can't make it work for him.

Because there's just nowhere for him to ply his trade. He can go again to the Gaslight for the – however many times –

Yes.

– but, you know, it's just going to get him the same results. He'll get some applause, he'll get drunk, and then the next morning he'll wake up on somebody's couch. As he does. The thing – and I'll say this. This is something I'll say about the film. This sounds like something a press agent would say, but I'll say it. I want to say this very soberly. I cannot think of a precedent in the history of civilization for this performance Oscar Isaac gives in this film.

Yes, he's amazing.

I don't think any actor has ever learned to play and sing a repertoire this thoroughly and compellingly and be able to film it all live without a click track, without the aid of tuning, without the aid of technology – just a complete analog performance of this character whose music Oscar had never heard a year before he did the film. Unbelievable. Oscar absorbed the guitar playing of Dave Van Ronk and the era – a technique known as Travis Picking – as if he was born to it. He learned all the songs, and he learned to sing 'em so naturally.

The thing is, when we were on the set – in the movie you always have some kind of thump track or click track or something that sets the tempo so you can cut between takes. But in this case, you know, the Coens decided early on that they just wanted to shoot and record the music live. No playback.

I was going to ask you about the decision to film the music live.

They wanted it that way, and because they wanted the movie to have something of a documentary feel, something of that period about it. I think they wanted the reality of it, just the raw reality of it happening right there because you can never get quite that thing in lip-synching. At any rate, I was talking about Oscar's performance. I was just sitting on the side – you know, just off-camera with this stop watch, old school, timing measures to see if Oscar was speeding up or slowing down. If we had a take or not that we could use. And Oscar never – he must have worked with a metronome or I don't know what. He's just got it in his soul. But he never varied once, not one song, on all those takes. He never, never varied. We were able to cut between every take. I'm excited about that 'cause there's just no better way to spend your time than doing this kind of thing that they do with this kind of music.

I understand that the Coens sent you Oscar's audition tape and you told them you felt he was as good as any professional musician in this music.

Yeah, I said he's as good as the musicians I work with – he's playing and singing as well as anybody I know. That style. And that's not an easy style to play. Travis Picking it's called, as I mentioned, it's a finger-picking style that was, as far as I know, pioneered by a black musician from Kentucky named Arnold Schultz who taught it to Ike Everly who taught it to Merle Travis, and then it became known as Travis Picking in Nashville because he popularized it.

Can I ask you about the music you chose for the film? Joel and Ethan, describing your working method together, said that they tell you what they're thinking and then you make suggestions. So can you talk a little about what you suggested and why for the film?

You know what? I can't remember – by the time we're finished, I'm serious, I look at it as such a collaboration that I don't distinguish between what anybody suggested other than I will say, honestly, I think they suggest almost everything. And I just facilitate. But, every once in a while I'll come up with something like maybe a good idea for another film or something. (*Laughs.*) Like on *The Big Lebowski* I suggested "Man of Constant Sorrow" as a, you know, a theme song for our epic hero, The Dude.

Yeah.

And they thought it was a great song for our epic hero Ulysses Everett McGill. In *O Brother, Where Art Thou?*

O Brother was their next film. They didn't use it in The Big Lebowski.

That's right . . .

They said you suggested "Five Hundred Miles," the Tom Paxton song, for Llewyn Davis.

I think I probably did. I love it – that's a beautiful, beautiful song. Dylan did a version of it. But the movie starts out with "Hang Me." Song about getting hung. And then it goes into "If I Had Wings," and then you come into Llewyn's world and you find the guy he had done "If I Had Wings" with jumped off a bridge. And then every song is either about death, abortion, murder, you know. It's separation. "Five Hundred Miles" I love because I think it's a slave song.

It is?

"I can't go home," you know, "I can't go home this way." It feels like a deep, beautiful song from the slavery era in this country, and I thought it was interesting the way it's been metabolized into the culture through folk music, the way I guess the liberal world was able to take that song and make it part of the culture in a way that people could hear it, you know, and not be too guilty. I don't know, I'm getting into some crazy territory . . .

It's very interesting. I love that song, but I never thought of it that way.

"If you miss the train I'm on, you'll know that I'm gone. Hundred miles . . . Not a shirt on my back, not a penny to my name, I can't go home this way." Doesn't that feel like that dislocation?

Yes.

That just feels like a deep story in our culture. An interesting aspect of the folk world is its connection to the Rights Movements, the Civil Rights Movement.

The progressive element of folk is emerging again at that time with people like Baez, and then Dylan appears. The Coens deliberately set the story specifically in the pre-Dylan era. They wanted to explore the music scene as they say that existed before Dylan came and changed everything.

In talking about the music in Inside Llewyn Davis *they said they see a deep connection to the music in* O Brother, *they say both films contain the same species of music. You feel that way as well?*

Yeah, I do. It's American, American music. Traditional – I call it traditional American music. I don't know what else to call it really because it's, it's the music of the poor people. And it's beautiful. Like all of the great cuisines, all the great food innovations – not all of them but so many of them – were peasant foods; barbecue for instance down here in the South. They invented barbecue sauce because they would get the meat that would go bad, and they'd have to cook it for two weeks to get it, to get it, you know . . .

Edible.

It would taste so bad they would put barbecue sauce, they'd put all kinds of crazy sauce on it. So that's this connection . . . to the kind of music this is. It's the kind of music that grows out of that same situation.

Can we talk a little more about the music in the film. That song, "Please, Mr. Kennedy." Where did that come from?

Well there was, there was a folk song during the Vietnam era called, "Please, Mr. Kennedy, Don't Send Me off to Vietnam." And my guess is it was a riff on a Tom Lehrer song. Tom Lehrer, the great satirist. I love Tom Lehrer. I think the folk movement took a cue from him and tried to produce that sort of satire. And that song, "Please, Mr. Kennedy" – it was supposed to be a fake rock 'n' roll song that was supposed to deal with the issue of Vietnam. But we moved it to our period and made it a spoof of the Space Race.

So it's a real song you just rewrote lyrics to?

Yes. We used the old song as a basis for this song, and then wrote new melodies and new lyrics. Justin [Timberlake] wrote a couple of new melodies, beautiful melodies, and I think all of us wrote lyrics. Justin, Ethan, Joel, and I all wrote.

You got Marcus Mumford of Mumford & Sons involved in the film, yes?

I did. 'Cause his music's quite interesting. He's the energy of his band, and the energy of that band is unbelievable.

I've never seen them live but I've got their albums on, you know, as you say, on the internet.

Marcus is really a brilliant and insightful lyricist, and I thought he was a good man. He just seemed like one of the boys. He seemed like he was on the team.

Let me ask you about Dave Van Ronk. Can you talk a little bit about him? I mean obviously you knew of him and the Coens knew of him.

Actually I didn't know him.

Really?

Yeah. The only thing I can tell you about Dave Van Ronk is he wasn't a loser. He was a brilliant artist who suffered this fate that many of us suffer. No matter what, you can suffer this fate . . . like in *Unforgiven* where the young kid has just shot a man and he's feeling incredibly guilty, and he's getting drunk, and he says, "Well he had it coming," and Clint Eastwood says, "We all got it coming, kid." It's a great line. But yeah, Dave never got his due, that's for sure. But you know, he was tremendously influential. You know Dylan slept on his couch. Like Llewyn, sleeping on couches. And like Llewyn, he never got his due. But he had it coming.